# Perishing

# Perishing

## What it means to lose the Life

Daniel R Shannon

**MENDING NETS**

Published by Mending Nets Ministries, Kaufman TX

www.hopeofglory.net

Cover by David Smith

ISBN: 979-8-9860819-4-6

Printed in USA

1st Edition

This work is dedicated to Lacy Evans. It only took me eight years or so to get this study to you.

Other books from Mending Nets:

Search the Scriptures
The Warnings in Hebrews

# Table of Contents

Introduction ........................................................................ 1

John 3:16 ........................................................................... 5

The Promise ..................................................................... 15

Zacchaeus and the Pounds ............................................. 31

Believers as Enemies ...................................................... 43

Many Will Perish ............................................................. 57

The Sheep Hear His Voice .............................................. 75

If We Hold Firmly to the Message .................................. 93

The Mystery of Lawlessness .......................................... 105

John 3:16 Revisited ....................................................... 115

Appendix 1 ..................................................................... 127

    Eternal Life ................................................................ 127

# Introduction

There is much said about perishing when talking to groups of believers. Many preachers expound upon the very real danger of perishing. Evangelists stand in the street and warn people about perishing. However, when it comes to be accepted into God's family through Christ, some teach that perishing means you are not in the family, others teach that it means you get kicked out of the family, while still others teach that you only thought you were in the family.

There is much confusion about what it means to perish.

Instead of relying upon opinions of others and commentaries of men, we need to let the Scriptures speak for themselves.

The goal of this study is to look at how the Bible uses the word "perishing" and how it should be applied. We want to teach you _**how**_ to study, not _**what**_ to think.

This study on perishing was originally one long study that was broken into bite-sized pieces for our Sunday school Bible study. We have attempted to present it as the original long study as it began, but broken into chapters that keep the individual ideas grouped together.

The translation that we have chosen to use is the New Revised Standard Version (NRSV). Unless otherwise noted, all passages are from the NRSV. Other translations that are used are the

Concordant Literal Version (CLV), Rotherham's Emphasized Version (REV), and the King James Version (KJV).[1]

All verses in the text are enclosed within brackets [ ]. Notes on the text (alternate meanings of words, expounded meanings of words, underlying words, etc.) are enclosed in brackets within the brackets. [[ ]].[2]

Have a grace day.

---

[1] The NRSV and KJV both let you know when something is changed in the text: The NRSV uses footnotes and the KJV uses italics. The KJV used footnotes in the older printings, but most modern printings omit translators' footnotes.

[2] Example: [1 John 1:9: *If* we confess [present; durative action; continually confess] our sins, he who is faithful and just will forgive us our sins [subjunctive; dependent upon if we confess] and cleanse us from all unrighteousness.]

# Perishing

# What It Means To Lose The Life

# John 3:16

[John 3:16 KJV: For God so loved the world, that he gave his only begotten Son, that whosoever believeth in him should not perish, but have eternal life.]

A little boy was overheard praying, "Lord, if you can't make me a better boy, don't worry about it. I'm having a real good time just like I am."

How many believers have this attitude today? They just want fire insurance and do not want to change their lives.

John 3:16 is a verse that we are all familiar with and we see many people using it as a common salvation verse. However, is that what it is? In our Bible study class, we were going to go into a study of the parables of Matthew 13, and as a foundation for that we decided it would be necessary to understand what it means to "perish" and to whom are the warnings about perishing applied.

[2 Peter 3:9: The Lord is not slow about his promise [*the* promise; singular], as some think of slowness, but is patient with you, not wanting any to perish, but all to come to repentance.]

This promise is singular. It does not say "promises". This is referring to something specific. "The promise" is talking about the inheritance that has been promised to Christians who live a faithful, obedient life.

So, to whom is this verse being written?

[2 Peter 1:1: Simeon Peter, a servant and apostle of Jesus Christ, To those who have received a faith as precious as ours through the righteousness of our God and Savior Jesus Christ:]

This passage is written to you and to me. He does not want any of those who have received a "faith as precious as ours" to perish, but come to [advance to] repentance. 2 Peter 3:9 is telling us that he does not want those who are in the family to perish (the word we are looking at) but wants us to change our course to the correct course.

[2 Peter 3:11-14: Since all these things are to be dissolved in this way, what sort of persons ought you to be in leading lives of holiness and godliness, waiting for and hastening the coming of the day of God, because of which the heavens will be set ablaze and dissolved, and the elements will melt with fire? But, in accordance with his promise, we wait for new heavens and a new earth, where righteousness is at home.]

This verse is talking about our lives and how we should be living lives of holiness and godliness. This is talking about works and it is a preparation for our future presentation at the Judgment Seat of Christ. Those who perish are those who will lose their lives. This can only be talking about someone who is in the family. Those who are not in the family are already dead in their trespasses and sins. They do not have a life to lose. You cannot lose something you do not have.

[Matthew 16:24-27: Then Jesus told his disciples, "If any want to become my followers, let them deny themselves and take up their cross and follow me. For those who want to save their life [soul] will lose it, and those who lose their life [soul] for my sake will find it. For what will it profit them if they gain the whole world but forfeit their life [soul]? Or what will they give in return for their life [soul]? "For the Son of Man is to come with his angels in the glory of his Father, and then he will ~~repay~~ pay everyone for what has been done.]

Denying ourselves is a contrast to what is next, which is a self-realization of our own plans and purposes. The word "life" is the same as the word "soul". The word "lose" is the same word we are looking at that is translated as "perish", and that is the word *apollumi*. If you save your life now, your life will perish, or you will lose your life in the future. If you disavow yourself and surrender your life now, you will gain life in the future.

He will pay everyone for what has been done. This is in reference to works. The wages of sin is death. The wages of righteous living is life in the age to come. We must destroy our self-willed ambitions and desires in this life, if we want to have life in the coming age. If we put ourselves aside today, we will enjoy the blessings of ruling and reigning and sharing in the glory of the Lord in that day.

"For what will it profit them if they gain the whole world but forfeit their life?"

This word "forfeit" is not the word *apollumi*. Let us take a look at another place with this word "forfeit".

[1 Corinthians 3:13-15: the work of each builder will become visible, for the Day will disclose it, because it will be revealed with fire, and the fire will test what sort of work each has done. If what has been built on the foundation survives, the builder will receive a reward. If the work is burned up, the builder will suffer loss; the builder will be saved, but only as through fire.]

In this verse, "suffer loss" is the same word as "forfeit".

One day, if you gain the entire world and everything it has to offer, you will lose. You will have no profit. The profit and loss statement will be in the red at the Judgment Seat.

This passage at which we are looking in Matthew 16 is not dealing with our common salvation; it is talking about works, discipleship, following the Lord, and the resulting rewards one day.

[Matthew 18:12-14: What do you think? If a shepherd has a hundred sheep, and one of them has gone astray, does he not leave the ninety-nine on the mountains and go in search of the one that went astray? And if he finds it, truly I tell you, he rejoices over it more than over the ninety-nine that never went astray. So it is not the will of your Father in heaven that one of these little ones should be lost.]

These are sheep – they have been in the fold – but they have gone astray. They are not sheep from outside the fold who just aimlessly wandered in. They have gone out of the fold. Where do the sheep go when they go astray? They wander off and get into trouble. They become influenced by demonic forces. They begin to serve the world, the flesh, and the Devil. As long as we serve the world, the flesh, and the devil, we are not in the fold. We are still sheep, but we are not in the fold.

There is an interesting phrase in this passage: "Gone astray".

[James 5:19-20: My brothers and sisters [brethren], if anyone among you wanders [goes astray] from the truth and is brought

Perishing

back by another, you should know that whoever brings back a sinner from wandering [straying] will save the sinner's soul from death [*thanatos*] and will cover a multitude of sins.]

These are sheep who go astray; they err. If they fall into error and are not __converted__, or brought back into the way, their soul will perish. If you convert a sinning brother, you will save a soul from death

[Hebrews 5:2: [The high priest] He is able to deal gently with the ignorant and wayward, since he himself is subject to weakness.]

Here, he deals gently with the wayward; those who are straying. This is a present, active verb; they are actively astray.

[Titus 3:3: For we ourselves were once foolish, disobedient, led astray, slaves to various passions and pleasures, passing our days in malice and envy, despicable, hating one another.]

This is what the straying sheep are doing while they are in the mountains wandering around. We were once led astray; we were deceived. This is not a reference back to our time prior to being born from above; we do not have the ability to be obedient or disobedient before we become believers. We had no life to lose!

Only one who has life can lose it. You cannot lose something you never had. You cannot lose a twenty dollar bill unless you first have a twenty dollar bill to lose.

This passage says we were sometimes foolish. We were living as if there were no God. We were deceived. We served our various passions.

9

Paul is warning Titus about the lifestyle of being disobedient, deceived, and serving self-pleasure, and all the malice and envy and being despicable and hating each other. There is a warning here: Those who live that way are in grave danger!

As we can see, "gone astray" means having been where you should be, but now being in error and being deceived.

[2 Peter 2:18-19: For they speak bombastic nonsense, and with licentious desires of the flesh they entice people who have just escaped from those who live in error. They promise them freedom, but they themselves are slaves of corruption; for people are slaves to whatever masters them.]

"In error" is the same word as "going astray".

[2 Peter 3:15b-16: So also our beloved brother Paul wrote to you according to the wisdom given him, speaking of this as he does in all his letters. There are some things in them hard to understand, which the ignorant and unstable twist to their own destruction, as they do the other scriptures.]

The things that Paul wrote about were even difficult for Peter to understand, and he spent a few years with Jesus! But look what he has to say about those who are ignorant and unstable: they twist the Bible in order to make it fit their own theology. They pick and choose the parts they like, and change the parts they dislike, or completely ignore parts of it altogether. They do not like what it says so they force it to say something else.

That is one reason more preachers no longer teach from the original languages: You can twist the English translation to make it say whatever you want. That is not quite so easy in the original languages, although it is obviously still possible since Peter is lamenting that situation.

It says they twist the words unto their own destruction: *apollumi*.

[2 Peter 3:17: You therefore, beloved, since you are forewarned, beware that you are not carried away with the error [straying] of the lawless and lose your own stability.]

Going astray means to be brought into error.

Let us look at the first time this word *apollumi* is used.

[Matthew 2:13: Now after they had left, an angel of the Lord appeared to Joseph in a dream and said, "Get up, take the child and his mother, and flee to Egypt, and remain there until I tell you; for Herod is about to search for the child, to destroy [*apollumi*] him."]

This is the way the word is first used.

[Luke 9:23-24: Then he said to them all, "If any want to become my followers, let them deny themselves and take up their cross daily and follow me. For those who want to save their life will lose it [future, active], and those who lose their life for my sake will save it [future, active].]

Any believer who puts himself first and the Lord second will perish in the age to come.

These warnings are given for one simple reason: we may fail to deny ourselves. We see this all over the world today. People are often taught the security of the believer, which is true, but no one teaches them about accountability. They come to a saving knowledge of the Lord, they proceed a little way into the deeper knowledge of the truth, and then they fall away when things get a little tough.

We might fail!

[Luke 9:25: What does it profit them if they gain the whole world, but lose [*apollumi*] or forfeit themselves?]

Here again we see the same word being used with forfeiting. He is disqualified. He will suffer loss. You can gain the whole world and yet still perish.

Those believers who have built their lives around wood, hay, and stubble will be in a heap of trouble at the Judgment Seat, but they shall be saved, so as through fire.[3] They are in the family, but there is no position of authority for them and no sharing in the glory of the Lord in his coming Kingdom. The hope of glory is not realized. Hope is not assurance, as so many errantly teach.[4]

[Luke 15:4: Which one of you, having a hundred sheep and losing one of them, does not leave the ninety-nine in the wilderness and go after the one that is lost until he finds it?]

They are in the wilderness among the mountains. Mountains have to do with heavenly things, and in the heavenlies is where our battle lies.

---

[3] See 1 Corinthians 3:10-15.
[4] In Acts 24, Felix hoped to receive money from Paul, but that did not happen.

# Perishing

[Psalm 121:1-2: I lift up my eyes to the hills—from where will my help come? My help comes from the LORD, who made heaven and earth.]

In the Hebrew, the implication of the phrasing is, "My help does not come from hills [satanic forces], my help comes from the Lord".

In the verse in Luke, the 99 are left in the wilderness, and he goes after the one that is perishing. *Apollumi.*

[Luke 15:7: Just so, I tell you, there will be more joy in heaven over one sinner who repents than over ninety-nine **_righteous_** persons who need no repentance.]

If you had $100,000 and you lost $1,000, you would turn your house upside to find the missing money. The $99,000 is secure, but you do not simply say to yourself, "$99,000 is enough." No! You want to find the missing money.

The sinner is an erring believer, not an unsaved person. He is a sheep who has gone astray. There is no such thing in the Bible as a "professor not a possessor". But what is a righteous person?

[Luke 1:6: Both of them [Zechariah and Elizabeth] were righteous before God, living blamelessly according to all the commandments and regulations of the Lord.]

This passage tells us what makes a person righteous: Knowing God's commandments and living that lifestyle. The ones who are living that lifestyle are the ones who will be found blameless at the Judgment Seat of Christ.

Who will be at the Judgment Seat of Christ? Only those who are in the family will be at the Judgment seat. They are the only one who have an inheritance at stake. This is a family matter. Sheep are a type of those who are holy; they are a type of those who are in the family.

# The Promise

[2 Peter 3:9: The Lord is not slow about his promise [the promise; singular], as some think of slowness, but is patient with you, not wanting any to perish, but all to come to repentance.]

We looked at this verse earlier. This promise is made to those who are in the family and it is talking about the promise. This is talking about an inheritance.[5] Perishing is losing the future life you could have and he is not wanting any to perish.

[Galatians 3:13-14: Christ redeemed us from the curse of the law by becoming a curse for us—for it is written, "Cursed is everyone who hangs on a tree"— in order that in Christ Jesus the blessing of Abraham might come to the Gentiles, so that we might receive the promise of the Spirit through faith.]

"In order that the blessing of Abraham might come to the Gentiles" does not make a reference to our common salvation being extended to the Gentiles; the Gentiles have always been able to be born from above into the family. This pertains to the promise that was made possible by the ministry of the Holy Spirt. The ministry of the Holy Spirit is a teaching ministry that reveals the deep things of God (*epignOsis*)[6], the deep things pertaining

---

[5] There are always two inheritances in view: The first is an inheritance that is given simply because someone is in the family. The better inheritance has to do with behavior.

[6] The word *"epignOsis"* means deeper knowledge. Not simply an understanding, but a much deeper understanding. It is literally knowledge upon knowledge.

15

to the mysteries of the Kingdom of the Heavens, and the things that pertain to ruling and reigning in that coming Kingdom.

The deliverance from the curse delivers the blessing to the Gentiles as well as the Jews.

[Galatians 3:18-19: For if the inheritance comes from the law, it no longer comes from the promise; but God granted it to Abraham through the promise. Why then the law? It was added because of transgressions, until the offspring [seed] would come to whom the promise had been made; and it was ordained through angels by a mediator.]

The inheritance belongs to the seed. Who or what is the seed?

[Galatians 3:16: Now the promises were made to Abraham and to his offspring; [seed] it does not say, "And to offsprings," [seeds] as of many; but it says, "And to your offspring," [seed] that is, to one person, who is Christ.]

The word "seed" is a collective noun. In other words, it refers to multiple units of the same type. (Not to be confused with *pluralia tantum*, which is a plural that is used as a singular, such as scissors[7], shorts, pants, etc.) However, just as in the English, when referring to an individual unit in the collective, it can be a single unit. In this case, there is much debate as to the meaning of "seed" and whether it is referring to a single unit or a single type.

For the answer to that, we need to turn to the passage that is being quoted and let Scripture interpret Scripture.

---

[7] Have you ever seen a scissor?

Perishing

[Genesis 22:15-18: The angel of the LORD called to Abraham a second time from heaven, and said, "By myself I have sworn, says the LORD: Because you have done this, and have not withheld your son, your only son, I will indeed bless you, and I will make your offspring [seed] as numerous as the stars of heaven and as the sand that is on the seashore. And your offspring [seed] shall possess the gate of their enemies, and by your offspring [seed] shall all the nations of the earth gain blessing for themselves, because you have obeyed my voice."]

In this passage, the word for "seed" (*zera* in the Hebrew), which is a collective noun, could be understood to refer to either Isaac and all his seed after him or it could refer to all Abraham's sons and their offspring such as the Ishmaelites, Edomites, Midianites, Israelites, etc.

The question that must be answered is, does "seed" refer to one specific line or to all of them?

[Genesis 17:18-21a: And Abraham said to God, "O that Ishmael might live in your sight!" God said, "No, but your wife Sarah shall bear you a son, and you shall name him Isaac. I will establish my covenant with him as an everlasting covenant for his offspring after him. As for Ishmael, I have heard you; I will bless him and make him fruitful and exceedingly numerous; he shall be the father of twelve princes, and I will make him a great nation. But my covenant I will establish with Isaac...]

Abraham asks for the blessing to be through Ishmael, but God says that although Ishmael will be blessed, the covenant [the LXX says it is an *aionian* covenant] will be made through Isaac.[8]

The type we are given that is being quoted by Paul is of a single unit: Isaac. Therefore in Galatians, the "seed" is also a single unit.

[Galatians 3:15-17: Brothers and sisters, I give an example from daily life: once a person's will [covenant] has been ratified, no one adds to it or annuls it. Now the promises were made to Abraham and to his offspring [seed]; it does not say, "And to offsprings," [seeds] as of many; but it says, "And to your offspring," [seed] that is, to one person, who is Christ. My point is this: the law, which came four hundred thirty years later, does not annul a covenant previously ratified by God, so as to nullify the promise.]

In other words, the inheritance belongs to the Lord Jesus Christ, and we can share in that inheritance.

[2 Peter 3:9: The Lord is not slow about his promise [*the* promise; something specific], as some think of slowness [not that he is unable to execute his promise], but is patient with you, not wanting [it is not his desire for] any to perish [*apollumi*], but all to come to repentance.]

The Lord is not unwilling to execute that promise. He is not wanting that any of us should perish, or lose our life in the age to come. He desires for all to grow into maturity and become responsible spiritual adults. He wants us to all be faithful so that

---

[8] See appendix 1 for a brief discussion on this word.

when we stand at the Judgment Seat of Christ, we may hear "Well done!"

[Luke 13:1-3: At that very time there were some present who told him about the Galileans whose blood Pilate had mingled with their sacrifices. He asked them, "Do you think that because these Galileans suffered in this way they were worse sinners than all other Galileans? No, I tell you; but unless you repent, you will all perish as they did.]

This is a passage that many evangelists (and other Christians) quote, and often (usually) quote out of context. It is often used in terms of repentance, but does not take into account the word "perishing" (*apollumi*) in verse 3. You will hear them raise their voice and emphasize, "My Bible says, except you repent, you shall likewise perish!" The point they are trying to make is, "unless you repent, you will not be saved".

Well, it does say that, but "likewise" (as they did) is the key word here. "You shall in like manner have your life taken from you." You too will be killed. That is what "likewise" (as they did) refers to here. It does not have anything to do with being born from above. It has to do with, "Unless you repent of your sins, you too will suffer the judgment of God."

The passage is talking about works and judgment, not "believe on the Lord Jesus". If you read verses 4 and 5, they are also talking about works. This is not talking about our common salvation.

[1 John 5:16-17: If you see your brother or sister committing what is not a mortal sin, you will ask, and God will give life to such a one—to those whose sin is not mortal. There is sin that is mortal; I do not say that you should pray about that. All wrongdoing [unrighteousness] is sin, but there is sin that is not mortal.]

There are believers who commit sins that are mortal sins; God will take them off the scene. Their labor and work, which is an embarrassment to the Lord is over and they will no longer embarrass the Lord with their sinful life and waywardness. These perish from the mortal life, but we are to be concerned with the ones that will cause us to perish in the age to come.

[Luke 15:4-7: "Which one of you, having a hundred sheep and losing one of them, does not leave the ninety-nine in the wilderness and go after the one that is lost until he finds it? When he has found it, he lays it on his shoulders and rejoices. And when he comes home, he calls together his friends and neighbors, saying to them, 'Rejoice with me, for I have found my sheep that was lost.' Just so, I tell you, there will be more joy in heaven over one sinner who repents than over ninety-nine righteous persons who need no repentance.]

Back to the sheep that go astray. This is talking about a sheep that is in the fold, having fellowship with the Shepherd and the other sheep, then he decides to go his own way. (In Matthew 18 he goes into the mountains.) This sheep comes under the influence of the world, the flesh, and the devil. The Shepherd finds that sheep and restores him into the fold.

The words "lose" and "loss" in verse 4 and the word "loss" in verse 6 are all "perishing" [*apollumi*] or losing one's life. Where it says, "there will be more joy in heaven over one sinner who repents", it is talking about saved sinners, not unsaved people. These are not people on their way to the lake of fire forever and ever. This has to do with believers who sin, repent, and return to the fold, compared to the 99 righteous people who need no repentance.

What is the definition of a righteous person who needs no repentance?

[Luke 1:6: Both of them [Zechariah and Elizabeth] were righteous [just] before God, living [walking or going] blamelessly according to all the commandments and regulations of the Lord.]

Zechariah and Elizabeth are both righteous. Why? Because they were walking according to the commandments and regulations of the Lord. They lived lives that were ordered according to the way they ought to be living. The ordinances of the Lord were part of their lives. A blameless life was the result of the way they lived.

"Walking" or "going" does not have to do merely with where you step; it is your way of life. It is a lifestyle!

Zechariah and Elizabeth needed no repentance.

The implication of perishing is that it is the result from the fact you are not walking in the commandments and ordinances of the Lord. This does not mean you need to be legalistic, but that you walk in the spirit of the Law.

Today we do not have to make sacrifices to atone for our shortcomings; the Lord took care of that on the cross. However, we are responsible for following the rules and running the race according to the rules.

21

We need to be righteous, just as Zechariah and Elizabeth were righteous.

What are the consequences of being unrighteous?

[1 Corinthians 6:9-10: Do you not know that wrongdoers [the unjust] will not inherit the kingdom of God? Do not be deceived! Fornicators, idolaters, adulterers, male prostitutes, sodomites, thieves, the greedy [covetous][9], drunkards, revilers, robbers— none of these will inherit the kingdom of God.]

These will not inherit. Inheritance is a family matter! This is not directed at those who are not in the family.

This word "wrongdoers" is the same word we are looking at; "righteous" or "just", but with the prefix "*a*" is added to it, making it the opposite; "unrighteous" or "unjust".

The sheep that has gone astray is an unjust or an unrighteous sheep. He is not behaving himself the way he ought to be behaving himself.

The consequences unrighteousness are that the unjust will not inherit the Kingdom of God.

"Do not be deceived! All these people will not inherit the Kingdom…"

-----

[9] This word seems to be overlooked by many evangelists when preaching against their favorite sins they like to condemn, but it is in all the "naughty" lists in the Bible. It is wanting that which does not rightfully belong to you. Our world is full of covetousness and our politicians are elected by those who want to take away from others and give it to them.

# Perishing

[1 Corinthians 6:11: And this is what some of you used to be. But you were washed, you were sanctified, you were justified in the name of the Lord Jesus Christ and in the Spirit of our God.]

When we get away from the commandments of the Lord and when we get away from the Word, we are vulnerable to going away into the mountains and falling into this list of sins. If we get away from the Word of God and his commandments, we can become all sorts of things; we can be influenced by the world, the flesh, and the Devil.

There are those who teach that someone who is really and truly saved cannot sin. Do not be fooled! There is not a sin in the book that a believer cannot commit!

The first step in the direction of unrighteousness is to get away from the Bible. This book will keep you away from sin or sin will keep you away from this book. That is the truth!

When you spend time in this book and you are having fellowship with those who love the Word, you are going to find positive encouragement to stay righteous. "Forsake not the assembling of yourselves together." It is more important as things get worse and you see the day approaching. As the end draws near, it is going to become more and more difficult to live an obedient Christian life. Persecution will increase for those who want to live righteous lives. If you believe in chastity and stand opposed to fornication and premarital sex, you will be ridiculed and you can even lose your employment.

[1 Corinthians 10:10-11: And do not complain as some of them did, and were destroyed by the destroyer. These things happened to them to serve as an example, and they were written down to instruct us, on whom the ends of the ages have come.]

The idea of the Bible keeping you safe is what Paul had in mind in this passage as well. When we read of OT types and examples as they pertain to believers, we see they were destroyed because of their behavior. What was their behavior?

[1 Corinthians 10:6-10: Now these things occurred as examples for us, so that we might not desire evil as they did. Do not become idolaters as some of them did; as it is written, "The people sat down to eat and drink, and they rose up to play." We must not indulge in sexual immorality as some of them did, and twenty-three thousand fell in a single day. We must not put Christ to the test, as some of them did, and were destroyed [perished; *apollumi*] by serpents. And do not complain as some of them did, and were destroyed [*apollumi*] by the destroyer.]

It is easy to eat and drink today. It is easy to play. Why? Because our society is built around fun and excitement. "If it feels good, do it." It is simple psychology that if you keep the people contented and distracted you can control them. Some of the most evil politicians in history understood that thoroughly, and the powers of darkness in politics today understand it thoroughly and buy votes so they can further erode liberty and righteousness.

We are living in an age in which we need encouragement from one another. We need encouragement, yet we often get discouragement, even (especially?) from those within the church. "Oh, you shouldn't take it so literally!" These things were given unto us to help us in these last time because it will be easy for us to become idolaters (covetous) and to lust after evil things. Think about the things the TV put before us as being "normal".

24

Perishing

Homosexuality is overrepresented, and that is one of the things that is "as it was in the days of Noah". The good shows are often inundated with evil advertising, and that is not a coincidence. If they cannot corrupt you directly, they will corrupt you indirectly. We need to be cautious about what we see because we can be drawn into those things; idolatry, fornication, murmuring, etc. The full list is a threat.

The sheep in the passage in Luke is an unjust sheep and he will not have an inheritance in the coming Kingdom; the sheep that is going astray is in danger of perishing; he will lose his life in the coming age.

Some of the sins in 1 Corinthians 10 were found in 1 Corinthians 6. If these sins are found in a believer's life, they will disqualify him from an inheritance in the coming Kingdom.

[Luke 15:8-10: "Or what woman having ten silver coins[10], if she loses [apollumi] one of them, does not light a lamp, sweep the house, and search carefully until she finds it? When she has found it, she calls together her friends and neighbors, saying, 'Rejoice with me, for I have found the coin that I had lost [apollumi].' Just so, I tell you, there is joy in the presence of the angels of God over one sinner who repents."]

[Luke 15:17: [The prodigal son was in the world, starving] But when he came to himself he said, 'How many of my father's hired hands have bread enough and to spare, but here I am dying [apollumi] of hunger!]

---

[10] Each coin is a drachma, which was about a day's pay for a laborer.

This is how the Holy Spirt deals with us when it comes to perishing. We are given a physical type in order that we may understand the spiritual type.

The son repented and went back to his father's house. The son was in the family, but had gone astray. He decided to go his own way and to eat, drink, and be merry. He had really been living it up, but now he was perishing. He repented and he **_returned_** to his father's house.

The woman had ten coins, but she lost one of them. Then she found the coin that was had already been hers. She did not find a new coin.

Heaven rejoices over the one sinner that repents more than the ninety-nine just ones. The woman found her lost coin. The son came to himself and said, "I have sinned", and the father received him and put him in the best robe, put a ring on his finger, shoes on his feet, and placed him in a place of honor in his home.

[Luke 15:24: for this son of mine was dead and is alive again; he was lost [apollumi] and is found!' And they began to celebrate.]

That is how it is in our Father's house!

[Luke 17:26-30: Just as it was in the days of Noah, so too it will be in the days of the Son of Man. They were eating and drinking, and marrying and being given in marriage, until the day Noah entered the ark, and the flood came and destroyed [apollumi] all of them. Likewise, just as it was in the days of Lot: they were eating and drinking, buying and selling, planting and building, but on the day that Lot left Sodom, it rained fire and sulfur from heaven and destroyed [*apollumi*] all of them—it will be like that on the day that the Son of Man is revealed.]

This is talking about the days of Noah and Lot.

[Luke 17:32: Remember Lot's wife.]

Why?

[Luke 17:33: Those who try to make their life secure will lose [*apollumi*] it, but those who lose [*apollumi*] their life will keep it.]

Lot's wife lost her inheritance; she looked back and turned into a pillar of salt.

This is terrible, right? It is not optimal, but it is not as bad as it could be. Salt is good until it loses its savor. If it loses its savor, then it is good for nothing but to be cast onto the dung pile.

[Hebrews 11:20: By faith Isaac invoked blessings for the future on Jacob and Esau.]

When you think of Lot's wife, you should think about Jacob and Esau. Esau was not an unsaved man. Esau is a picture of a believer who lives in the world and lives for the world.

Legally, Esau's name should be listed first; the firstborn son's name is always listed first. However, Esau was disqualified from the inheritance of the firstborn. That is why we find Jacob's name first; Jacob received the birthright of the firstborn. But let us not forget that Esau received a blessing as well. He forfeited the better inheritance, but there is an inheritance we receive simply for being in the family.

[Hebrews 12:16-17: See to it that no one becomes like Esau, an immoral and godless person, who sold his birthright for a single meal. You know that later, when he wanted to inherit the blessing, he was rejected, for he found no chance to repent [change his father's mind], even though he sought the blessing with tears.]

Esau committed the sin unto death. He lost the life he could have had. He committed the unpardonable sin. He sold his birthright. He had no regard for his inheritance. He still received an inheritance, but he forfeited the inheritance of the firstborn. He forfeited the blessings for position, authority, and rewards.

There is more to the backstory than the few sentences given in this passage. This passage was written to those who would be expected to know the backstory. If we know the background, we know that when Esau went out hunting, he was hunting Nimrod. Mainly because Nimrod was hunting him, but Esau was successful in that hunt and Nimrod's men were coming after him. He did not have enough faith in God to protect him and he felt that his birthright would not be any good, so he made a contract to sell his birthright to his brother and that bowl of soup sealed the contract.[11]

------

[11] Esau also desired to rule the world and stole Nimrod's clothing which was the clothing God had made for Adam, which would have given him that power and authority. If Esau had been successful in ruling the world, he would have had no need for his birthright, therefore he despised it on two counts.

# Perishing

Esau did not esteem the better inheritance and he forfeited it. Jacob esteemed these things and got them.

Esau sought to regain these forfeited things with tears; he wept when he found out what he had lost!

There is going to be weeping at the Judgment Seat of Christ because many will have lost their lives in the age to come because they wanted to eat, drink, and be merry in this life. Because they want to live it up today, they will lose in the coming age! Saved, yes, but disqualified to rule and reign.

[Luke 17:32-33a: Remember Lot's wife. Those who try to make their life secure will lose it [_**will**_ perish]...]

This verb is indicative; they _**will**_ perish. Their life will be lost.

This has to do with life in the coming age. It has to do with honor and glory and sharing in the inheritance of the Lord.

[Luke 17:33b: ...but those who lose [_apollumi_] their life will keep it.]

This is not talking about suicide. This is talking about those who put their selfish ambitions to death today.

[Colossians 3:5: Put to death, therefore, whatever in you is earthly: fornication, impurity, passion, evil desire, and greed [covetousness] (which is idolatry).]

We are exhorted to destroy these things in our lives in order that we may seek those things which are from heaven! If we lose our lives today, we will find our lives in the age to come.

[Luke 19:10: For the Son of Man came to seek out and to save the lost [perishing; *apollumi*]].

[Luke 19:26-27: I tell you, to all those who have, more will be given; but from those who have nothing, even what they have will be taken away. But as for these enemies of mine who did not want me to be king over them—bring them here and slaughter them in my presence.]

# Zacchaeus and the Pounds

Let us revisit 2 Peter 3:9.

[2 Peter 3:9: The Lord is not slow about his promise [the promise; singular], as some think of slowness, but is patient with you, not wanting any to perish, but all to come to repentance.]

So far, we have established that those who have not accepted the Lord Jesus as their personal savior are already dead in their trespasses and sins, therefore, they cannot perish. Only someone who has something to lose can lose it; therefore, only those who have life can perish.

When we see the word "perish" (or perishing), we need to associate with those who are born from above; those who have life.[12] This is not talking about losing your common salvation; that can never, under any circumstance, be lost, neither can it be forfeited.

[Luke 19:1-10: He entered Jericho and was passing through it. A man was there named Zacchaeus; he was a chief tax collector and was rich. He was trying to see who Jesus was, but on account of the crowd he could not, because he was short in stature. So he ran ahead and climbed a sycamore tree to see him, because he was

---

[12] Unless, of course, the passage is dealing with physical perishing, such as the case of Herod trying to destroy Jesus in Matthew 2:13, which says: Now after they had left, an angel of the Lord appeared to Joseph in a dream and said, "Get up, take the child and his mother, and flee to Egypt, and remain there until I tell you; for Herod is about to search for the child, to destroy him."

going to pass that way. When Jesus came to the place, he looked up and said to him, "Zacchaeus, hurry and come down; for I must stay at your house today." So he hurried down and was happy to welcome him. All who saw it began to grumble and said, "He has gone to be the guest of one who is a sinner." Zacchaeus stood there and said to the Lord, "Look, half of my possessions, Lord, I will give to the poor; and if I have defrauded anyone of anything, I will pay back four times as much." Then Jesus said to him, "Today salvation has come to this house, because he too is a son of Abraham. For the Son of Man came to seek out and to save the lost [perishing; *apollumi*]."]

We are going to look at the story of Zacchaeus, then look at the parable of the pounds. These two stories go together. We are going to look at perishing in these passages, then we are going to look at the context and correlation.

[Luke 19:10: For the Son of Man came to seek out and to save the lost [perishing; *apollumi*]."]

Verse 2 tells us that he was rich. Verse 3 tells us that he was a wee little man, but he wanted to see Jesus, so in verse 4, he climbed up a sycamore tree.

[Luke 19:5-9: When Jesus came to the place, he looked up and said to him, "Zacchaeus, hurry and come down; for I must stay at your house today." So he hurried down and was happy to welcome him. All who saw it began to grumble and said, "He has gone to be the guest of one who is a sinner." Zacchaeus stood there and said to the Lord, "Look, half of my possessions, Lord, I will give to the poor; and if I have defrauded anyone of anything, I will pay back four times as much." Then Jesus said to him, "Today salvation has come to this house, because he too is a son of Abraham.]

This passage can be taken in two different ways: Either Zacchaeus was a man who had already been born from above but was interested in Jesus, or he was an unsaved man prior to this event. If he were an unsaved man, he already had all the information he needed; he just did not have the faith.

Grammatically, I believe he was unsaved because in verse 6, he "was happy to welcome him" [received him joyously]. "Received" is an aorist verb, and I believe this indicates that this is when he applied his knowledge and believed.[13]

However, "joyously" is a present, active verb.

Because Zacchaeus already had the knowledge, he went straight from infancy to living faithfully. Jesus never made any reference to the common salvation, but does make reference to salvation after Zacchaeus *did* something. This is about works.

Our common salvation is not based on works. Without faith, our works are as filthy rags. There is nothing we can do to deserve our common salvation or nothing we can do of our own power to make us worthy of receiving rewards. Only when we act by faith are our works worthy, and apparently, Zacchaeus's works were faithful.

---

[13] I would like to point out that this is a matter of semantics. For the purpose of the following discussion, it does not matter if this was the initial salvation event or not.

[Luke 19:8: Zacchaeus stood there and said to the Lord, "Look, half of my possessions, Lord, I will give to the poor; and if I have defrauded anyone of anything, I will pay back four times as much."]

Zacchaeus really repented. He is going to give to the poor, and "if I have defrauded, I will pay back four fold".

The way this admission is worded, it is assumed to be true. He is not stating a subjective claim (if I have defrauded, as an uncertainty), but by the grammar, he is stating, "those whom I have defrauded, I will restore four fold".

Tax collectors had to purchase their tax territory. They were responsible for collecting a certain amount in taxes, and everything else was theirs to keep. Many tax collectors got wealthy that way, and Zacchaeus was wealthy, so it is a safe assumption that extortion is how he got wealthy. Paying taxes is not evil, but extortion is. This is not the only place that Jesus confronts extortion.

[Luke 3:14: Soldiers also asked him, "And we, what should we do?" He said to them, "Do not extort money from anyone by threats or false accusation, and be satisfied with your wages."]

"What should we do?" This would have been the perfect opportunity for Jesus to say, "Throw down your swords and quit soldiering" if he thought being a soldier was inherently sinful. However, he tells them to not extort money and be content with what they have earned. Soldiers were notorious for saying, "Pay me or I will say you did so-and-so and take you in". That is evil. Being a soldier is not evil.

# Perishing

After Zacchaeus repents what does Jesus say?

[Luke 19:9b-10: "Today salvation has come to this house, because he too is a son of Abraham. For the Son of Man came to seek out and to save the lost [perishing; *apollumi*]."][14]

Zacchaeus responds and repents in a way that puts him on a path for positions of authority in the coming Kingdom. He does something [works] and Jesus responds and says, "He too is a son of Abraham."

[Galatians 3:7, 29: so, you see, those who believe are the descendants [sons] of Abraham...And if you belong to Christ, then you are Abraham's offspring [seed], heirs according to the promise.]

Zacchaeus was a son of Abraham. Abraham had two seeds. Before this event, Zacchaeus was already a seed of Abraham physically (as sands on the seashore); after this event, he was a son of Abraham spiritually (as stars in the sky).

This is implying inheritance, and there are always two inheritances in view: One inheritance that is by birth and one that is earned. The inheritance that is earned is based upon works performed under grace. If they are not performed in grace, no matter how "good" they may be, they are by nature, works of wood, hay, and stubble.

---

[14] It is important to remember that "salvation" has more than one meaning, and Abraham had more than one seed. "Salvation" is not always the born-from-above-into-the-family salvation. See the book The Warnings in Hebrews, Adoption, and Why We Are All Going to Hell by the same author for a thorough discussion on this.

So, Zacchaeus repented and salvation came to his house.

Then what?

[Luke 19:11-14: As they were listening to this, he went on to tell a parable, because he was near Jerusalem, and because they supposed that the kingdom of God was to appear immediately. So he said, "A nobleman went to a distant country to get royal power for himself and then return. He summoned ten of his slaves, and gave them ten pounds, [15] and said to them, 'Do business with these until I come back.' But the citizens of his country hated him and sent a delegation after him, saying, 'We do not want this man to rule over us.']

His own citizens rebelled and said they would not have this man to rule over them!

[Luke 19:15: When he returned, having received royal power [having obtained the Kingdom], he ordered these slaves, to whom he had given the money, to be summoned so that he might find out what they had gained by trading.]

Once again, works are in view. "What did you do to profit with what I gave you?"

This parable has to do with the coming Kingdom; it has to do with profit and loss with the investment that has been given to his servants. This is about the stewardship of what these servants have been given!

---

[15] *Mina*; about three months' wages for a laborer.

Perishing

This passage denies the legitimacy of so-called Christian socialism. Capitalism is presented in the light of a positive attribute. The Holy Spirit is not going to use something evil to explain something that is good. In other words, he will not say, "Socialism is the right way, but we are going to use the concept of capitalism, which is evil, to explain how you are supposed to do things". The very concept of socialism, as a form of government was forbidden in the commandment, "Thou shall not steal". We are to work in the physical world and we are to work in the spiritual world.

[Luke 19:16-17: The first came forward and said, 'Lord, your pound has made ten more pounds.' He said to him, 'Well done, good slave! Because you have been trustworthy in a very small thing, take charge of ten cities.']

This is talking about a trustworthy [faithful] servant. This is about works. This is the Lord of lords and King of kings providing himself with lords and kings. If he is the Lord of lords and King of kings, then he must have lords and kings to be over.

Here, we have a faithful servant who is given authority over ten cities.

[Luke 19:18-21: Then the second came, saying, 'Lord, your pound has made five pounds.' He said to him, 'And you, rule over five cities.' Then the other came, saying, 'Lord, here is your pound. I wrapped it up in a piece of cloth [napkin], for I was afraid of you, because you are a harsh man; you take what you did not deposit, and reap what you did not sow.']

Here, we have an unfaithful servant.

The unfaithful servant puts his pound in a napkin.

The word "napkin" is found elsewhere in relation to Jesus.

[John 20:6-7: Then Simon Peter came, following him, and went into the tomb. He saw the linen wrappings lying there, and the cloth [napkin] that had been on Jesus' head, not lying with the linen wrappings but rolled up in a place by itself.]

This word "napkin" is found in only four verses in the Bible.

We have these passages in Luke 19:20 and John 20:7. In John 11:44, Lazarus came forth from the tomb, and the napkin is referred to as a separate piece of cloth. It is also found in Acts 19:12.

[Acts 19:12: God did extraordinary miracles through Paul, so that when the handkerchiefs [napkin] or aprons that had touched his skin were brought to the sick, their diseases left them, and the evil spirits came out of them.]

In every case, this word has to do with grave clothes, after a fashion. The napkin is associated with death or perishing.

The important thing in this passage in Luke 19:20-21 is that this *is* a servant. He may be a wicked servant, but he *is a servant*!

This wicked servant did not actively do anything evil; he simply did not do anything. This wicked servant simply wrapped his pound in dead works and placed it in the ground.

When you think of the napkin, you should think of grave clothes and dead works that are placed aside. When you think of Lazarus, think upon the fact that the Lord Jesus raised him from the dead, but He had others roll aside the stone and take away the grave clothes. We all have to help each other in taking off dead works.

[Luke 19:21-22a: for I was afraid of you, because you are a harsh man; you take what you did not deposit, and reap what you did not sow.' He said to him, 'I will judge you by your own words, you wicked slave [servant]!]

This title "wicked servant" is used in a few different places in the Bible.

[Matthew 13:47-50: "Again, the kingdom of heaven is like a net that was thrown into the sea and caught fish of every kind; when it was full, they drew it ashore, sat down, and put the good into baskets but threw out the bad. So it will be at the end of the age. The angels will come out and separate the evil from the righteous and throw them into the furnace of fire, where there will be weeping and gnashing of teeth.]

We have already looked at those who are just; they live blamelessly before the Lord in keeping his commandments. In this passage, the wicked are severed from the just.

Many people say this is the separating the saved in one direction and the unsaved in another. That is not accurate! This has to do with the Kingdom, which is the rule of the heavens over the earth, and that will happen at the end of this age as we go into the next age, or the age to come. Notice that in verse 50, there will be weeping and gnashing of teeth. There will be disappointment and frustration for those who realize what they have lost and what they could have had. They have come up short for qualifications for ruling and reigning with the Lord in the coming Kingdom.

[Matthew 18:23-35: "For this reason the kingdom of heaven may be compared to a king who wished to settle accounts with his slaves. When he began the reckoning, one who owed him ten thousand talents[16] was brought to him; and, as he could not pay, his lord ordered him to be sold, together with his wife and children and all his possessions, and payment to be made. So the slave fell on his knees before him, saying, 'Have patience with me, and I will pay you everything.' And out of pity for him, the lord of that slave released him and forgave him the debt. But that same slave, as he went out, came upon one of his fellow slaves who owed him a hundred denarii[17]; and seizing him by the throat, he said, 'Pay what you owe.' Then his fellow slave fell down and pleaded with him, 'Have patience with me, and I will pay you.' But he refused; then he went and threw him into prison until he would pay the debt. When his fellow slaves saw what had happened, they were greatly distressed, and they went and reported to their lord all that had taken place. Then his lord summoned him and said to him, 'You wicked slave! I forgave you all that debt because you pleaded with me. Should you not have had mercy on your fellow slave, as I had mercy on you?' And in anger his lord handed him over to be tortured until he would pay his entire debt. So my heavenly Father will also do to every one of you, if you do not forgive your brother or sister from your heart."]

This is a parable about an unmerciful servant. This parable shows us an unforgiving spirit. In this passage, a person who has an unforgiving spirit is called a "wicked servant".

---

[16] A talent was fifteen years' wages for a laborer.
[17] A day's wages for a laborer.

# Perishing

[Matthew 25:24-30: Then the one who had received the one talent also came forward, saying, 'Master, I knew that you were a harsh man, reaping where you did not sow, and gathering where you did not scatter seed; so I was afraid, and I went and hid your talent in the ground. Here you have what is yours.' But his master replied, 'You wicked and lazy slave! You knew, did you, that I reap where I did not sow, and gather where I did not scatter? Then you ought to have invested my money with the bankers, and on my return I would have received what was my own with interest. So take the talent from him, and give it to the one with the ten talents. For to all those who have, more will be given, and they will have an abundance; but from those who have nothing, even what they have will be taken away. As for this worthless slave, throw him into the outer darkness, where there will be weeping and gnashing of teeth.']

Here, we have the parable of the talents, which is given as a follow up to the parable of the virgins. What happened to the wicked and lazy servant? He received no positive reward! He did not lose anything; he simply did not gain anything. He was thrown into a place that was separated from the glory of the coming Kingdom.

[Hebrews 3:12: Take care, brothers and sisters, that none of you may have an evil [wicked], unbelieving heart that turns away from the living God.]

Here again we find the word wicked. This has to do with a heart of unbelief[18], which is talking about the children of Israel because

---

[18] This is an unbelieving heart; an unfaithful heart. See the study on "Faith or Believe". This expression "evil heart" appears in only a few places, and most of those places are in the Apocrypha.

of their wicked heart. This is because of the unfaithfulness of Israel and their departing from the Lord. That is what happens when we are unfaithful. To repeat: Either the Bible will keep us from sin or the sin will keep us from the Bible.

[Luke 19:23-26: Why then did you not put my money into the bank? Then when I returned, I could have collected it with interest.' He said to the bystanders, 'Take the pound from him and give it to the one who has ten pounds.' (And they said to him, 'Lord, he has ten pounds!') 'I tell you, to all those who have, more will be given; but from those who have nothing, even what they have will be taken away.]

The servant who hid his pound in a napkin is referred to as one of unbelief or lack of faith. Unbelief is timid faith, not a complete lack of faith. Then, we have an exhortation and a promise in this passage.

If there is no profit, then that **_which he has_** is taken away and given to the one who has earned ten pounds! This cannot be talking about common salvation because that **_cannot be taken away!_**

However, in this passage, even that which he has (which was given to him, not earned) is taken away, and given to another. This is where the idea of a double portion comes into play.

The double portion of the inheritance has to do with what the Lord takes away from the unfaithful and gives to the faithful. He takes away that which he had entrusted to them and gives it to those who have been faithful with that which they had been entrusted.

# Believers as Enemies

[Luke 19:27: But as for these enemies of mine who did not want me to be king over them—bring them here and slaughter them in my presence.]

This is the part that a lot of preachers like to skip over. This part is rough. This is where we find those who are believers who are also his enemies.[19]

[James 4:4: Adulterers! Do you not know that friendship with the world is enmity with God? Therefore whoever wishes to be a friend of the world becomes an enemy of God.]

This disturbs many people because it shows who God's enemies really are. There are plenty of Christians (and plenty of churches) that are very friendly with the world; they "tolerate" and even embrace all sorts of evil. They are close friends with the world. The real enemy is the one who would rather have friendship with the world than have the Lord reign over him. Our true enemy will not let the Lord have dominion. The enemy will not be led of the Holy Spirit.

These enemies are associated with the house of Israel because of Luke 19:14, but it also applies to all believers today. When the Lord was on the Earth, only Israel could qualify to rule and reign, that has been taken away, and now anyone can qualify: The Gentiles as well as the Samaritans can now qualify.

---

[19] As Napoleon Bonaparte once said, "Never interrupt your enemy when he is making a mistake."

[Galatians 3:29: And if you belong to Christ, then you are Abraham's offspring [seed], heirs according to the promise.]

If we will not allow the Lord to rule over our life, we _**will**_ lose our life.

This is what happens at the Judgment Seat of Christ. At the Judgment Seat of Christ, the faithful and unfaithful believers are judged. It is not a judgment of whether or not you are in the family. _**All**_ believers will appear at the Judgment Seat, and _**only**_ believers will be there.

[Luke 19:27: But as for these enemies of mine who did not want me to be king over them—bring them here and slaughter them in my presence.]

They lose their lives at the Judgment Seat.

[Luke 19:10: For the Son of Man came to seek out and to save the lost [perishing; _apollumi_].]

We will take a deep look at John 3:16 at the end of this study, but let us take a brief look at it now. Many people use this verse as a salvation verse, but that is an error on multiple levels.

[John 3:16 KJV: For God so loved the world, that he gave his only begotten Son, that whosoever believeth in him should not perish, but [may] have ~~everlasting~~ _aionian_ life.]

I chose to use the KJV for this verse because it is the one most people are familiar with due to seeing it at all the sporting events. This phrase, "should not perish", is subjunctive. The word "should" in English is properly subjunctive, particularly when the KJV was translated, as opposed to "would", and the underlying Greek word is subjunctive.[20] That means that it is one removed from the indicative. In the Greek, there is indicative, subjunctive, optative, and imperative.

Indicative means there is no doubt about it

[Acts 16:30-31: Then he brought them outside and said, "Sirs, what must I do to be saved?" They answered, "Believe on the Lord Jesus, and you will be saved, you and your household."]

"Believe on the Lord Jesus and you _will_ be saved". That is indicative. It is simply a statement of fact.

Subjunctive means that it is probable success but there is the possibility of failure. For example, someone goes shopping and says, "I don't plan on buying anything more than the necessities".

"What must I do to be saved?" Or, literally, "what must I do that I may be being saved?" What is my salvation dependent upon? That is the subjunctive because it may not succeed because the result is dependent upon the action of "believe"; the individual may or may not believe.

---

[20] The common usage of "should" rarely retains the correct usage of this word in modern English. Also, while there is a distinction between "will" and "shall", one of those differences is to indicate a first person future action. In other words, "shall" is usually subjunctive except in certain circumstances. This is one reason that it is often more accurate to go to the underlying language instead of making a guess at what the translators were after.

[Acts 27:12: Since the harbor was not suitable for spending the winter, the majority was in favor of putting to sea from there, on the chance that somehow they could reach Phoenix, where they could spend the winter. It was a harbor of Crete, facing southwest and northwest.]

The optative is what Paul used when they were traveling from Crete and he said in this passage "on the chance that somehow they could reach Phoenix". What happened? They did not winter there and they shipwrecked in Malta. This shows how the optative is used.

The imperative gives no indication of the fulfillment of action of the verb. The imperative is just a command and there is no guarantee that that command will ever be carried out. Acts 16:31 says, "***Believe*** on the Lord Jesus and you will be saved". "Believe" is in the imperative; it is a command but there is no indication of fulfillment. You may either believe or not.

If you believe on the Lord Jesus you will be saved. Period. There is no wiggle room there.

In John 3 we find two aspects of the love of God demonstrated.

[John 3:16b: ...whosoever believeth in him should not [subjunctive] perish, but [may] have ~~everlasting~~ *aionian* life.]

Those who believe in the present tense (those who are faithful) may or may not perish, but if they continue to be faithful they may have *aionian* life. If they cease to continue in faithfulness, they may not have *aionian* life. There is a second subjunctive verb they KJV omits from the text and this leads to confusion and misuse of the text. Being in the family is no guarantee that you will rule and reign; have *aionian* life.

In the first part of John 3:16, we see the love that God had for the world. God loved the world so much that he sent the Lamb of God to die that all men might be saved. In the second part, he expresses the desire and made the provision for believers that they might not perish. We see both John 3:3 and John 3:5 in John 3:16.

[John 3:3: Jesus answered him, "Very truly, I tell you, no one can see the kingdom of God without being born from above."].

Some translation say "born again", however, "born from above" is more accurate and is less confusing. The word is the same word as "above" in John 3:31. Also, when the Lord Jesus Christ was crucified, the veil in the temple was rent from above to the bottom. So, the birth here is from above; being born from above. This is being placed into the family of God. And everyone who is placed into the family of God is going to be able to see the Kingdom.

There are several Greek words for the word "see". One has to do with a worship or involved observation, and then there is this word, which is the word for the simple mechanical idea of seeing something. In this case, it has to do with seeing the activities of the Kingdom.

When you merely see the Kingdom, there is no participation or direct involvement. There is simply casual observation. Along with that casual observation there may be some weeping and gnashing of teeth to go with it, for those who are not qualified to enter in, but this verse is talking about simply seeing. God has provided provision for the whole world. He has provided the means for everyone to be born from above. "Behold the lamb of God, which taketh away the sin of the world." Christ died that all men might be saved.

[John 3:5: Jesus answered, "Very truly, I tell you, no one can enter the kingdom of God without being born [again] of water and Spirit.]

This verse says "enter". There is a difference between seeing and entering. I can see into a car, but until I qualify by unlocking and opening the door and crawling in, I cannot enter. I can simply see a football game, even though I may be on the team. There are plenty of people who have seen a football game. Even if I am on the team, if I am sitting on the 3rd string, I may be sitting on the bench. But the 1st stringers get to play; they are the ones who are qualified to enter in. And that is how it is going to be in the Kingdom. There are going to be spectators, 2nd and 3rd stringers, and there will be the starting lineup.

The ones who do not enter – the ones who do not qualify to rule and reign – they are the ones who perish or lose their life. They did not successfully follow the rules.

The word "water" is literal because the word "spirit" is literal. This is a compound prepositional phrase, and the preposition that rules those two nouns means that you have to take them both figuratively or both literally. This has to do with baptism and being filled and led of the spirit; it has to do with being influenced by the teaching ministry of the Holy Spirit.

Anyone who has not been baptized will not be qualified to enter in. Refusal of baptism is direct disobedience. That is the reason the children of Israel could not enter Canaan – they were living in open disobedience.

John 3:5 deals with qualifications of entering in to rule and reign with the Lord. This leads up to the second part of John 3:16.

[John 3:14-15: And just as Moses lifted up the serpent in the wilderness, so must the Son of Man be lifted up, that whoever believes in him may have ~~eternal~~ *aionian* life.]

[Numbers 21:4: From Mount Hor they set out by the way to the Red Sea, to go around the land of Edom; but the people became impatient on the way.]

"They" are the children of Israel. These are God's people. They are not unsaved people who are not in the family. They were discouraged. These are the ones that came out of Egypt, all being baptized in the sea and in the cloud unto Moses.

[Numbers 21:5: The people spoke against God and against Moses, "Why have you brought us up out of Egypt to die in the wilderness? For there is no food and no water, and we detest this miserable food."]

These people began to hate what God provided them. If you look at the manna they were loathing, it was a type and picture of the Word of God. They loathed the Word of God. Think how you would feel if you invited someone over to dinner every day for several years, then one day they stood up and said, "We loathe these steak and potatoes". (This verse literally says, "Our soul is irritated by this lightly esteemed bread".)

49

[Numbers 21:6: Then the LORD sent poisonous [fiery] serpents among the people, and they bit the people, so that many Israelites died.]

They perished.

[1 Corinthians 10:9: We must not put Christ to the test, as some of them did, and were destroyed [*apollumi*] by serpents.]

Those who fell in the wilderness did not enter into Canaan. They lost their lives. This may be hard to take, but even though Moses did not fall because of a serpent bite (he was not bitten by a fiery serpent), Moses did perish in the latter end of his life because of unbelief. He fell just like those who were bitten by the fiery serpents fell in the wilderness.[21]

[1 Corinthians 10:10: And do not complain as some of them did, and were destroyed [*apollumi*] by the destroyer.]

The word "destroyed" is "perished"; perished by serpents; *apollumi*.[22]

[1 Corinthians 10:2-5: and all were baptized into Moses in the cloud and in the sea, and all ate the same spiritual food, and all drank the same spiritual drink. For they drank from the spiritual rock that followed them, and the rock was Christ. Nevertheless,

---

[21] There are those who believe, with good justification, the serpents are "fiery" not because of their bite but because of their color, hence the brass serpent on the pole would match their color. Remember also that in the Bible, brass is the color or metal of judgment.

[22] "The Destroyer" is a different word than *apollumi* and is more appropriately translated as "the exterminator". I actually like the phrase, "destroyed by the exterminator".

God was not pleased with most of them, and they were struck down in the wilderness.]

These are the ones who perished by serpents. They were all baptized in the cloud and the sea, at the same spiritual food, and drank the same spiritual drink.

[Numbers 21:7-9: The people came to Moses and said, "We have sinned by speaking against the LORD and against you; pray to the LORD to take away the serpents from us." So Moses prayed for the people. And the LORD said to Moses, "Make a poisonous serpent, and set it on a pole; and everyone who is bitten shall look at it and live." So Moses made a serpent of bronze, and put it upon a pole; and whenever a serpent bit someone, that person would look at the serpent of bronze and live.]

Moses made the serpent of brass. Brass represents judgment. He lifted the serpent on a pole. Jesus had taken on the judgment of the world when he was lifted on a pole. God had already judged the Lord Jesus Christ when he raised him again into the heavenlies. This fiery serpent that Moses lifted up was the means whereby the children of Israel who had murmured against the Lord could keep from perishing. All they had to do was to choose to look upon the fiery serpent. And in typical fashion, they later turned this serpent on a pole into an idol.[23]

Right now, the Lord Jesus Christ has been raised into the heavenlies. He is our high priest. To keep from perishing – to

---

[23] How do you treat the cross on your church building or the crucifix on the chain? Is it merely a symbol to let others know where you stand or have you turned it into an idol?

keep from losing our lives – we have to look up and appropriate the high priestly office of Jesus Christ in the heavenlies.

[Philippians 3:10-11: I want to know Christ and the power of his resurrection and the sharing of his sufferings by becoming like him in his death, if somehow I may attain the resurrection from [among] the dead.]

"That I may know him, and the power of his resurrection…" Paul was not interested in knowing the Lord on just a casual basis, he was interested in knowing the Lord Jesus Christ in the power of His resurrection, because he hopes to attain to the out-resurrection from among the dead ones. From among those who have perished. Paul was interested in being raised from among the dead ones. That gives you the story.

[Luke 14:11: For all who exalt themselves will be humbled, and those who humble themselves will be exalted.]

This word "exalt" is the same word that is translated as "lifted up" in our passage in John.

[John 3:14-15: And just as Moses lifted up the serpent in the wilderness, so must the Son of Man be lifted up, that whoever believes in him may have ~~eternal~~ *aionian* life.]

Moses exalted the Lord Jesus Christ in type when he lifted up the serpent on the pole.

[Acts 2:32-33: This Jesus God raised up [different word], and of that all of us are witnesses. Being therefore ***exalted at the right hand of God***, and having received from the Father the promise of the Holy Spirit, he has poured out this that you both see and hear.]

This is where Jesus is today. He is exalted to the right hand of God. He was raised up from among the dead.

[Acts 5:30-31: The God of our ancestors raised up [roused; not the same word as exalted] Jesus, whom you had killed by hanging him on a tree. God exalted him at his right hand as Leader and Savior that he might give repentance to Israel and forgiveness of sins.]

[Acts 13:17: The God of this people Israel chose our ancestors and made the people great [exalted the people] during their stay in the land of Egypt, and with uplifted arm he led them out of it.]

[Romans 4:25: who was handed over to death for our trespasses and was raised for our justification.]

The Lord Jesus has been resurrected and has been lifted up or exalted to the right hand of the Father and he is there interceding for us in order that we might be justified and qualify to rule and reign from the heavens.

[John 3:15: that whoever believes in him may have ~~eternal~~ *aionian* life.][24]

"Whoever believes…" is a participle, which is a verb used as a noun. It is present, active and is singular. A literal translation

---

[24] "Should not perish" does not belong in this verse according to most texts and manuscripts. It seems to be a late addition.

would be, "in order that everyone, the one believing". "Believe", as a present, active, participle, is synonymous with "faith", which is a lifestyle. This is talking about continual faithfulness and confidence in God. This is not the on-again off-again go-to-church-on-Easter-and-Mother's-Day type of belief. This is not, "I think I will trust the Lord today, but if tomorrow doesn't go my way, I might not". This is not talking about the security of a believer; this is talking about someone who is being faithful in order that they may have *aionian* life. The security of the believer is referenced elsewhere in the indicative, which is the Greek verb that means there is no doubt about it. *Aionian* life has to do with life in the coming age. Here, "may have *aionian* life" is subjunctive, which means there is the possibility of failure.

There are warnings throughout the NT warning us that we may fail to enter into God's rest, and those are very real warnings. But those warnings ***never*** extend to our ultimate security.

The entire concept is contingent upon the present tense of the verb "believe"; it has to do with our faithfulness to God. The security of the believer depends upon God's faithfulness to the believer, and God's faithfulness never fails.

Our qualification for ruling and reigning (*aionian* life) depends upon our faithfulness to access the throne of grace where we find the blood for deliverance and grace in order that our service is made acceptable. If we fail to do this and go off into the error of what seems right in our own way, we will not qualify to rule and reign with the Lord, and therefore we will perish and lose our life in the age to come.

We find the same verbs in verse 16. When the Holy Spirit had John write 3:14-16, He was saying, "I want you to remember

54

what happened to Moses and the children of Israel in the desert so you can apply it to John 3:16". Why do we know that? Because the verb tenses in John 3:16 are the same as in 3:15.

[John 3:16 KJV: For God so loved the world, that he gave his only begotten Son, that whosoever believeth in him should not perish, but have everlasting [*aionian*] life.]

"For God so loved the world, that he gave his only begotten Son, that whosoever **believeth**..." The word "believeth" is a present active participle. It is identical to what is in verse 15. The one who is continually putting his confidence in the Lord and putting those thoughts into action. "Should not perish..." The one who is continually faithful should not perish. But he might perish if he fails to continue in faithfulness. Still in the family? Yes! But not in a position of authority. "But **may** have *aionian* life". He may not have. It is contingent upon the faithfulness of the one who is believing.

Traditions and the teachings of man have so distorted this passage that it is nearly impossible to get past the preconceived ideas that are so ingrained into to us. Because of the preformed and pre-thought-out theology, most preachers and teachers refuse to teach from the Greek because the Greek is **accurate** and it does not always mesh with what they **want** it to say. If they were to go into the Greek, this verse would not fit into their pre-existing theology, and that is hard on the ego and it does not tickle the ears.

The security of the believer is true. However, John 3:16 does not teach that. In order to get security out of John 3:16, you must ignore the Greek because it is not there. God's desire is that every individual might repent and live a life of obedience in order that they may have life in the coming age.

# Many Will Perish

[2 Peter 3:9: The Lord is not slow about his promise, as some think of slowness, but is patient with you, not wanting any to perish, but all to come to repentance.]

Not wanting or not intending any to perish. We know from 2 Peter 3:7 that many will perish, but that is not what God wants.

[2 Peter 3:7: But by the same word the present heavens and earth have been reserved for fire, being kept until the day of judgment and destruction of the godless.]

He desires all to come to repentance, but it is the individual's choice and responsibility. We are not automatons.

"The Lord is not slow about his promise…"

The promise is singular. What is that promise?

[1 John 2:25 CLV: And this is the promise which He promises us: the life [the] eonian [aionian].]

This is *the* life *the* aionian. Both "life" and "age-lasting" have the definite article. This is not simply talking about our common salvation. This has to do with ruling and reigning [the life] in the coming age.

Since we have covered a lot of ground, I want to do a brief summary of what we have studied up until this point, with a few additions.

In John 3:3 we saw that in order to **see** the Kingdom, one must be born from above. But, John 3:5 tells us that in order to enter into the things pertaining to the Kingdom, one must be born again of water and spirit. John 3:3 is the first birth from the perspective of a believer, while John 3:5 is another beginning.

[1 Peter 1:3: Blessed be the God and Father of our Lord Jesus Christ! By his great mercy he has given us a new birth into a living hope through the resurrection of Jesus Christ from the dead.]

God the Father has begotten us again (a new birth). He begot us the first time in John 3:3 from above. Then he begets us again unto a living hope. That living hope has to do with ruling and reigning. We do not hope we have been born into the family, but we hope that we can remain faithful. Those who have eyes to see and ears to hear are the ones who respond to that message. This is the pearl of great price.

So, John 3:5 has a new beginning for believers.

[Romans 6:4: Therefore we have been buried with him by baptism into death, so that, just as Christ was raised from the dead by the glory of the Father, so we too might walk in newness of life.]

In John 3:5 both water and spirit are literal. Baptism is necessary for ruling and reigning. Since this is a compound prepositional phrase, both water and spirit must be literal or both must be spiritualized. If you want to spiritualize the water, then you must spiritualize the spirt, and that is just plain silly.

Romans 6:4 shows what is in John 3:5, in that it is a second birth in which we are raised again in newness of life. This is a new life or a new way of living.

[John 12:24-26: Very truly, I tell you, unless a grain of wheat falls into the earth and dies, it remains just a single grain; ***but if it dies***, it bears much fruit. Those who love their life lose it, and those who hate their life in this world will keep it for eternal life. Whoever serves me must follow me, and where I am, there will my servant be also. Whoever serves me, the Father will honor.]

[Colossians 3:1-5a: So if you have been raised with Christ, seek the things that are above, where Christ is, seated at the right hand of God. Set your minds on things that are above, not on things that are on earth, for you have died, and your life is hidden with Christ in God. When Christ who is your life is revealed, then you also will be revealed with him in glory. ***Put to death, therefore, whatever in you is earthly***: fornication, impurity, passion, evil desire, and greed (which is idolatry).][25]

These passages are talking about dying to one's self. The KJV says "mortify therefore your members" and "mortify" literally means to put to death. This is a way to look at baptism. Baptism is symbolic of death to self, and you are raised to newness of life. After baptism, you are walking with the Lord, seeking those

---

[25] The KJV has "covetousness" instead of "greed". "Greed" is correct here. Greed is a strong desire for something, but covetousness implies that it is something that belongs to someone else. Greed implies that you are putting whatever it is you desire above God. There is nothing wrong with wealth or goods, but that desire can become an all-consuming desire and it becomes idolatry. Covetousness is always wrong.

things, which are above. Or at least that is what you should be doing.

This is what is contained in John 3:3 and 3:5. John 3:3 is talking about being saved or being born from above. Then, in John 3:5, it says, "no one can enter the kingdom of God without being born of water and Spirit.". This is not talking about simply being born from above, it is talking about an entrance into and involvement in the things pertaining to the Kingdom of the Heavens.

No one that has not been baptized will be qualified to enter in. To refuse baptism is direct and visibly open disobedience to the commands of God. That is the reason the children of Israel could not enter Canaan; they were living in open and direct disobedience. John 3:5 deals with qualifications of entering in to rule and reign with the Lord.

[John 3:14-15: And just as Moses lifted up the serpent in the wilderness, so must the Son of Man be lifted up, that whoever believes in him may have eternal life.]

If you think back, this raising up of the serpent was drawing upon a story from the period when the children of Israel were in the wilderness.

[Numbers 21:4: From Mount Hor they set out by the way to the Red Sea, to go around the land of Edom; but the people became impatient on the way.]

God's people came out of Egypt, were baptized in the sea and in the cloud. In type, they are those who are born from above.

Perishing

[Numbers 21:5: The people spoke against God and against Moses, "Why have you brought us up out of Egypt to die in the wilderness? For there is no food and no water, and we detest this miserable food."]

They were discouraged and they began to hate what God provided them, which was a type of the Word of God. Then, one day they stood up and said, "We loathe this food which has no substance or nutritive quality". Yet it sustained them in the desert forty years. We do the same thing: We are always wanting something "better" than what we have instead of wanting the things of God.

[Numbers 21:6: Then the LORD sent poisonous [fiery] serpents among the people, and they bit the people, so that many Israelites died.]

They perished.

Those who fell in the wilderness were in the land of promise, but not the land of the better promise, the Land Flowing with Milk and Honey. They lost their lives. Even though Moses was not bitten, he **_did_** perish in the latter end of his life because of unbelief.

[1 Corinthians 10:9: And do not complain as some of them did, and were destroyed by the destroyer.]

[KJV 1 Corinthians 10:9: Neither let us tempt Christ, as some of them also tempted, and were destroyed of serpents.]

In the NRSV, this verse does not state the full impact of what is being said. It says, "Let us not put the Lord on trial". Let us not

61

"tempt out" or "tempt thoroughly". It is a compound word that is very significant and is used only in three other places, all of which have to do with putting the Lord on trial.[26] Let us not tempt Christ, for if we do, we will be destroyed by serpents. We will be perished by serpents. *Apollumi.*

When the children of Israel were in the wilderness, those who put the Lord on trial were perished by serpents. In order to change course, they had to change where they were looking so Moses made a brass serpent for them to look upon as opposed to the fiery serpents that were besetting them.

[Numbers 21:7-9: The people came to Moses and said, "We have sinned by speaking against the LORD and against you; pray to the LORD to take away the serpents from us." So Moses prayed for the people. And the LORD said to Moses, "Make a poisonous [fiery; brass] serpent, and set it on a pole; and everyone who is bitten shall look at it and live." So Moses made a serpent of bronze, and put it upon a pole; and whenever a serpent bit someone, that person would look at the serpent of bronze and live.]

Moses made the serpent of brass and lifted it up on a pole. Throughout Scripture, brass is a picture of the judgment of God. God had already judged the Lord Jesus Christ when he raised him again into the heavenlies. Right now, the Lord Jesus Christ is raised into the heavenlies. He is exalted. He is our high priest today. To keep from perishing (to keep from losing our life) we must appropriate the high priestly office of Jesus Christ in the heavenlies. We need to gaze upon him. This brings us back to the present in our study.

---

[26] Matthew 4:7, Luke 4:12, and Luke 10:25.

Perishing

[Philippians 3:10-11: I want to know Christ and the power of his
resurrection and the sharing of his sufferings by becoming like
him in his death, if somehow I may attain the resurrection from
[among] the dead.]

Paul was not simply interested in knowing the Lord on a casual
basis, he was interested in knowing the Lord Jesus Christ in the
power of the resurrection. Literally, the out-resurrection from
among the dead ones. Paul was interested in being raised from
among the dead ones.

[John 3:14-15: And just as Moses lifted up the serpent in the
wilderness, so must the Son of Man be lifted up, that whoever
believes in him may have eternal life.]

Remember, "lifted up" is the same as "exalted". Moses exalted
the Lord Jesus in type when he lifted up the serpent on the pole.

[Luke 14:11: For all who exalt themselves will be humbled, and
those who humble themselves will be exalted.]

[Acts 2:32-33a: This Jesus God raised up [different word], and
of that all of us are witnesses. Being therefore ***exalted at the right
hand of God***...]

That is where he is today, exalted at the right hand of God after
God raised him up from among the dead, and this is what Paul is
referring to when he says, "That I may know him, and the power
of his resurrection.

[1Peter 1:3: Blessed be the God and Father of our Lord Jesus
Christ! By his great mercy he has given us a new birth [born

63

again, not born from above] into a living hope through the resurrection of Jesus Christ from [among] the dead.]

We are born from above when we believe. We are born again through the resurrection of Jesus Christ from among the dead. This is how we can realize our living hope: Through (and by means of) the resurrection of the Lord Jesus.

[John 3:16 KJV: For God so loved the world, that he gave his only begotten Son, that whosoever believeth in him should not perish, but have everlasting [*aionian*] life.]

In the first part, God loved and God gave. "For God so loved the world that he gave." Both of these verbs are active, indicative. God was active in loving and giving, and the indicative means there is no doubt about his loving and giving. It is a simple statement of fact. God loved and God gave.

Then it says, "Whosoever believeth on him;" literally, "the one that is believing". This verb is a present, active, participle. The individual is active in the believing and it is durative in action, not an event. "The one who continues actively believing."

For someone to be born from above into the family of God, that action is not durative, it is aorist; it is an event. In Acts 16:31, the jailor had to believe and he was in the family of God. The aorist tense is punctiliar action. Believe and you are in the family.

However, not everyone who is in the family is faithful. We all have times of unfaithfulness, but where is our heart? We are sometimes lax. We are not steadfast as we should be. We are not unmovable. We fluctuate. That is why we have a way out.

# Perishing

[1John 1:9: If we confess our sins, he who is faithful and just will forgive us our sins and cleanse us from all unrighteousness.]

*If* we confess our sins, he is faithful and just to forgive us. If we do not confess, he does not cease being faithful and just and we will be held accountable. Thank God that even though we may not be faithful his is always faithful! We can wipe the slate clean. We get a do over.

In John 3:16, those who are believing **_should_** not perish, but **_may_** have *aionian* life.

Both "should not be perishing" and "may have" are subjunctive. There is the possibility that we might perish and that we might not have life for the coming age. The action is contingent upon our faithfulness. "Believe" in the present tense is synonymous with the noun "faith". If we are believing we should not perish, but we may stop being faithful.

[Matthew 7:13-14: Enter through the narrow gate; for the gate is wide and the road is easy that leads to destruction, and there are many who take it. For the gate is narrow and the road is hard that leads to life, and there are few who find it.]

We are going to look at some passages that have to do with "everlasting (or eternal) life". I want you to appreciate that this expression pertains to life for the coming age. The word "everlasting" is from "*aionian*", from which we get "age".[27] The word life is "*zoe*".

---

[27] This is not bad translating, it is simply that we have changed the way we use this word in the English language and we try to apply a modern meaning to an old word.

This passage in Matthew 7 shows the word "life" as it pertains with the walk of a believer. Someone who is in the family and is interested in life for the coming age is going to enter in at the narrow gate. The broad way is the easy way to go through this life, but when we enter into battle with satanic forces, we are going to be pressed in. We will have conflict and opposition. However, successfully resisting the conflict and opposition will lead to life for the coming age.

[Mark 10:17: As he was setting out on a journey, a man ran up and knelt before him, and asked him, "Good Teacher, what must I do to inherit eternal [*aionian*] life?"]

The first clue in this verse is the word "inherit". This lets you know this is someone who is in the family. Inheritance is a family matter. He is concerned with what his inheritance will be. He is not worried about whether or not he is in the family; he knows if he is in the family. But he is concerned with his inheritance in the age to come.

[Mark 10:21-22: Jesus, looking at him, loved him and said, "You lack one thing; go, sell what you own, and give ~~the money~~ to the poor, and you will have treasure in heaven; then come, follow me." When he heard this, he was shocked and went away grieving, for he had many possessions.]

This man is rich and his riches cause him to stumble and to forfeit his inheritance. This passage is talking about rewards. "Treasure in heaven" has to do with your inheritance in the age to some. It is not the wealth that is the problem, it is the position the wealth holds in his life. It causes him to not live by faith.

"Follow me" is service. It is works. That was the problem. He was serving his money rather than serving the Lord. He was not dying to self. We must serve the Lord if we want to lay up treasure in heaven. Sometimes that might mean selling what we own if our stuff is a stumbling block in our lives.

[Mark 10:28-31: Peter began to say to him, "Look, *we have left everything* and *followed you.*" Jesus said, "Truly I tell you, there is no one who has left house or brothers or sisters or mother or father or children or fields, for my sake and for the sake of the good news [gospel], who will not receive a hundredfold now in this age—houses, brothers and sisters, mothers and children, and fields, with *persecutions*—and in the age to come eternal [*aionian*] life. But many who are first will be last, and the last will be first."]

In verse 28, Peter says, "We gave up everything" and verse 30 tells us that he shall receive an hundred fold of houses, brethren, mothers and children, and fields... and then the part that people do not like: with persecutions. If you are faithful you will have opposition. There will be trouble.

But if you do these things, in age to come, *aionian* life. You will have life!

Right now we are living in the age of grace. We are in the church age. The age to come is the millennial age. It will be the age of the glory of the Lord. If we are faithful now, we can have life – we can rule and reign – in the age to come. That is our hope of glory!

[Luke 18:28-30: Then Peter said, "Look, we have left our homes and followed you." And he said to them, "Truly I tell you, there is no one who has left house or wife or brothers or parents or children, for the sake of the kingdom of God, who will not get back very much more in this age, and in the age to come eternal [*aionian*] life."]

When you see works involved, the subject is not our common salvation. There are no works on our part for the common salvation. This has to do with inheritance. This has to do with rewards. Everyone in the family has an inheritance, but some will have a better inheritance than others. This is about *aionian* life in the Millennial age.

[1 John 5:11-13: And this is the testimony: God gave us eternal life, and this life is in his Son. Whoever has the Son has life; whoever does not have the Son of God does not have life. I write these things to you who believe [are believing] in the name of the Son of God, so that you may know that you have eternal life.]

"Believe" in verse 13 is a present, active, participle. It is durative action, not aorist. These are the ones who are faithful. "That you may know" is subjunctive. This book is written to believers who are faithful in their walk, so that you may know that you have life for the coming age and that you may continue to believe on the name of the Son of God. We believe as an event to be born from above; we continue believing to be faithful.

Many, if not most, look at this passage as referring to common salvation, or being born from above. However, verse 13 tells us to whom he is writing. They are already believers. If you were trying to get people saved into the family, you would not be talking to people who are already believers. What he is saying here is, "I have written unto those of you who are believing on the name of the Son of God that you may know that you have life in the age to come and that you may continue in your faithfulness and confidence on the Lord and continue to believe on the name of the Son of God".

[Titus 1:1-2: Paul, a servant of God and an apostle of Jesus Christ, for the sake of the faith of God's elect [this is written to those who are called out] and the knowledge [*epignOsis*; deeper knowledge] of the truth that is in accordance with godliness, in the __*hope*__ of eternal [*aionian*] life that God, who never lies, promised before the ages began...]

The promise of God is life for the coming age. He does not will any of us to perish but that we all come to repentance that we might experience and enter in to that promise.

We see the word "hope" used with *aionian* life. As far as our common salvation (born from above) is concerned, we do not hope that we are in the family of God. We __*know*__ we are in the family of God because we have believed.

If you try to apply this passage to common salvation, you are going to have to twist it in order to make it fit your preconceived theological positions. To do that, you are going to have to distort what it says. You are going to have to twist and distort the very meaning of the word "hope". To hope for something means, "to look forward to something, with implication of confidence about something coming to pass, or to look forward to something in view of the measures one takes to ensure fulfillment".[28] And you do not hope for your common salvation.

---

[28] BDAG.

However, there is hope associated with an entrance or ruling and reigning.

[Titus 3:7: so that, having been justified by his grace, we might become [subjunctive] heirs according to the hope of eternal [*aionian*] life.]

Being justified, we **_might be_** made heirs. This phrase is subjunctive. Our inheritance is based on the hope. The word "according to" is the Greek word "*kata*" and it means "in the dominion of" and in this case, it is in the dominion of the hope that we have as far as life for the coming age is concerned. It is not hope of our common salvation, it is a hope that we may find ourselves approved.

[Romans 2:6-10: For he will repay according to each one's **_deeds_** [works or acts]: to those who by patiently doing good seek for glory and honor and immortality, he will give eternal [*aionian*] life; while for those who are self-seeking and who obey not the truth but wickedness, there will be wrath and fury. There will be anguish and distress for everyone who does evil, the Jew first and also the Greek, but glory and honor and peace for everyone who does good, the Jew first and also the Greek.]

Works are associate with life for the coming age. There are no works on our part for our common salvation either to get saved, stay saved, or to prove we are saved. Works are works are works! Works have to do with rewards in the coming Kingdom. Works have to do with *aionian* life.

This word "immortality" is the word "incorruption". These are believers within the family, not the unsaved outside the family. They are "patiently doing good". This is the same idea in the verb in John 3:16: believing, faithfulness, or steadfastness. It is endurance. These are ones in the family who endure to seek glory, honor, and incorruption and will therefore receive *aionian* life in the age to come.

When works are involved, it is not talking about common salvation. When works are involved, it is the individual's responsibility to seek after these things faithfully and in obedience to the Word of God.

[James 1:12: Blessed is anyone who endures [present, active] temptation [testing or trial; it is singular]. Such a one has stood the test [different word] and will receive the crown of life that the Lord has promised to those who love [present, active] him.]

Here, anyone who endures testing has stood the test. It is the word "*dokimos*" and means "approved". The one who endures will be found approved and will receive a victor's crown of ***the life*** that has been promised to those who continually love him. This is a "*stephanos*" crown; it is a victor's crown that is not a sovereign crown, it is earned.

[1 Corinthians 9:24: Do you not know that in a race the runners all compete, but only one receives the prize? Run in such a way that you may win it.]

We run to obtain a victor's crown. James is telling us that the one who endures to the end will be found approved and he ***will*** receive the victor's crown of the life in the coming age which the Lord has promised to those who are loving him continually. If he endures, he will be rewarded.

If you love him, you will keep his commandments. If you love him, you will be obedient. If you do not love him, you will not keep his commandments and you will be a disobedient servant and you will miss out on the crown of life and you will not rule and reign with him in the heaven. You will perish at the Judgment Seat of Christ. The exhortation is to lose your life now in order that you might have life in the coming age. If you realize your life today, you will perish in ***that*** day and you will not enter into life.

*Aionian* life is life in the coming age. It is not the common salvation. The common salvation is secure for the believer. If you believe, you are in the family and you cannot be unborn. You can, however, forfeit the life you might have one day.

Consistency in the scriptures is important. As we saw in 2 Peter 3:9, the author included himself in the possibility of perishing, yet people try to apply the passage to the common salvation which is irrevocable and secure. They create an inconsistency that is not native to the text. Only those who have life can perish and those who are unsaved have no life to lose. They are already dead in their trespasses and sins.[29]

When we study, consistency is imperative because inconsistency creates unnecessary confusion for many people. Inconsistency is one reason there are so many denominations. There are some denominations that believe baptism is necessary for common salvation. That is called baptismal regeneration. Baptism is necessary for salvation of the soul, but the only thing necessary for common salvation is "believe on the Lord Jesus". Baptism is necessary if you are interested in ruling and reigning.

---

[29] Ephesians 2:1.

One thing that causes problems for many people is that there are some passages that say if you do certain works you will be saved. This leads to the Arminian view that as long as we are being good, we will make it into heaven. We are on the road. We are on the gospel train. We have our hand on the throttle. The Pilgrim's Progress is a prime example of Arminian doctrine. It teaches that if we can keep on the narrow path and hang on and pray through, then we will make it to the sweet by and by.

This creates an inconsistency in the Bible. This is why we are studying the word "perish". If there are inconsistencies, the inconsistencies are with the way men handle the Word, they are not in the Word itself. The words of God are accurate and the Word of God is accurate!

# What It Means To Lose The Life

# The Sheep Hear His Voice

The Lord is not slack concerning **_the_** promise, which is enjoying a full allotment in the age to come. If we perish, we will lose the life we could have had.

[John 10:27-28: My sheep hear [present, active] my voice. I know them, and they follow me. I give them eternal [*aionian*] life, and they will never [*ou mE*][30] perish. No one will snatch them out of my hand.]

This is talking about sheep. This is referring to believers who are actively hearing his voice.

[John 10:2-3a: The one who enters by the gate is the shepherd of the sheep. The gatekeeper opens the gate for him, and the sheep hear [present, active] his voice.]

"Hear" is present, active. This is durative action. This is not an on again, off again situation where they listen when they feel like it. They continually **_hear_**! This can be compared to continually studying and growing in the grace and knowledge of the Lord. Continually growing in the knowledge of God is how we have grace and peace.

[2 Peter 1:2: May grace and peace be yours in abundance in the knowledge [*epignOsis*] of God and of Jesus our Lord.]

---

[30] This is a double negative. In the Greek, it does not negate itself, it is an emphatic **_never_**.

[John 10:3b-4: He calls his own sheep by name and leads them out. When he has brought out all his own, he goes ahead of them, and the sheep follow [present, active] him because they know his voice.]

Here we find works. Entrance in and out and following the shepherd because they know his voice. They are *listening* and they are *following.*

[John 10:27: My sheep hear my voice. I know [am knowing] them, and they follow [are following] me.]

This passage gives reference to those whom he knows. Does he not know everyone?

[Matthew 7:21: "Not everyone who says to me, 'Lord, Lord,' will enter the kingdom of heaven, but only the one who does the will of my Father in heaven.]

This passage is dealing with an entrance into the coming Kingdom of the Heavens. This is referring to some who seem to think they deserve an entrance.

[Matthew 7:22-23: On that day many will say to me, 'Lord, Lord, did we not prophesy in your name, and cast out demons in your name, and do many deeds of power in your name?' Then I will declare to them, 'I never knew you; go away from me, you evildoers.']

They did might works! When they said, "did we not do all this mighty stuff", he did not reply, "You did not!" They did these things. But these things were not the will of the Father in heaven. It is more important to be obedient than to be mighty. Sometimes the Lord just wants you to sit still. It does not matter how good the works are that you do, if you do them under your own authority, they are not obedience.

The Lord calls them "workers of iniquity". The NRSV translates it as "you evildoers", which is accurate, but it does not give the full impact. They are workers of lawlessness. They are doing what is right in their own eyes. They will be popular preachers with their congregations. And one day they will be very surprised.

It says, "I never knew you". He obviously knows them, but he does not _**know**_ them. He does not acknowledge them as doing what they are supposed to be doing.[31]

[John 10:27: My sheep hear my voice. I know [am knowing] them, and they follow [are following] me.]

"I know them." The ones who listen to him and are obedient, he acknowledges. These are the ones who will have an entrance. These are the ones who will rule and reign.

[John 12:25a: Those who love [present, active] their life lose it [present active]...]

He who is loving his life is perishing. If you love your life in this age, you are perishing and you will not have a life in the age to come.

---

[31] We may do this with our children on occasion. "You did what? Who are you? I don't know you." We obviously know who they are, but we do not acknowledge and approve of their behavior.

[John 12:25-26: Those who love their life lose it, and those who hate their life in this world will keep it for eternal [*aionian*] life. Whoever serves me must follow me, and where I am, there will my servant be also. Whoever serves me, the Father will honor.]

Following the Lord is works. The word "follow" is a present, active and it is middle voice. The middle voice means it is something you cause to happen for yourself. Following has to do with service, not merely tagging along. Service will result in the father honoring you. God the father will honor a person who follows the Lord.

[John 10:27: My sheep hear my voice. I know them, and they follow me.]

"They are following me." "Follow" is present, active. There is no fluctuating, they are following constantly. There is no doubt in their minds who the shepherd is. This is a reference to mature believers who have a hope of ruling and reigning. They are faithful.[32]

[John 10:28: I give them eternal [*aionian*] life, and they will ~~never perish~~ not perish into the age. No one will snatch them out of my hand.]

I am giving them life for the age. When we compare scripture with scripture, we know we can forfeit ruling and reigning in the coming age, but we know we cannot forfeit our common salvation. In this passage, life for the age to come is offered to us,

---

[32] Numbers 18:17 tells us that sheep are holy animals. When you see sheep, it is not an unsaved person. And unsaved person is not holy. Also keep in mind that goats are holy as you study the Bible.

based upon the present tense of following or being faithful. If we are going to be faithful in hearing, and following, and service, we can expect God to honor us in the coming age. That is what God has done with his Son. He has honored the Son with glory, power, and dominion in the coming Kingdom, and we can be part of that!

"And they will not perish into the age." Even though the present tense if found all throughout this passage, there is a double negative "*ou mE*" here in the Greek. Unlike English (technically, unlike bad English), in Greek the double negative does not negate something, it is an emphatic negative. Never, never perish.

"Perish" is subjunctive, however. The Lord wants to remind us that there is the possibility of failure on our part. If we are faithful, we will **_not_** perish, but there is the possibility that we can fall short. Keep this in your mind: if there were no possibility of perishing, there would be no warning. If every believer were going to rule and reign, there would be no warnings. If every believer were going to have equal outcomes, there would be no warnings. If every believer did not commit certain sins, there would be no warnings. If not for the possibility of failure, the Bible would only need one verse in it: "Believe on the Lord Jesus and you will be saved." If there were no possibility of failure, there would be no perishing, therefore there would be no need of warnings, and the Bible would simply need to list all the neat stuff we can expect to get when get there.

But that is not what the Bible does. The Bible continually warns believers, over and over and over, not to do certain things. Not because we can become unsaved and not be part of the family of God, but as an exhortation to be faithful in our walk in order to have honor and glory in the coming Kingdom.

Those who continually hear his voice and follow and serve him will never perish. It is contingent. As soon as you quit listening and quit following and serving, you cannot expect the Father to honor you. That is why the word "perish" is subjunctive: You might fail in your faithfulness.

[1 Corinthians 1:18: For the message about the cross is foolishness to those who are perishing, but to us who are being saved it is the power of God.]

Every word is here for a reason and the accuracy of the verbs is important. Always remember, "Words mean things". "The message about the cross is foolishness to those who are perishing..." This is present, passive. These are ones who are in the process of being perished. "But to us who are being saved..." This is also present, passive. For those of us who are in the process of working out our salvation, this message is the _**power**_ of God.

[Philippians 3:18: For many live as enemies of the cross of Christ; I have often told you of them, and now I tell you even with tears.]

Paul makes reference to believers who are the enemies of the cross of Christ. He is not referencing those who are outside the family, but those who are in the family but are unfaithful.

[Philippians 3:11-14: if somehow I may attain the _**out-**_ resurrection from the dead. Not that I have already obtained this or have already reached the goal; but I press on to make it my own, because Christ Jesus has made me his own. ~~Beloved~~ Brethren, I do not consider that I have made it my own; but this one thing I do: forgetting what lies behind and straining forward to what lies ahead, I press on toward the goal for the prize of the heavenly call [up-calling] of God in Christ Jesus.]

This passage is dealing with the prize and the high calling or up-calling of God in Christ Jesus. This is a calling to come up above those believers who are perishing. This is talking about the out-resurrection from among the dead.

Paul, the apostle who was taught face-to-face by Jesus uses the subjunctive. "If somehow I may attain the out-resurrection..." He admits the possibility of failure. And then he says that he has not obtained this or reached the goal. But he presses on to make it his own because Jesus Christ has made him his own. He wants to rule and reign but Paul is emphasizing here that we might attain that, but then again, we might not.

Remember, the out-resurrection is talking about those believers who lose their life in the coming age. Paul is not trying to instill fear in us that we might miss the resurrection or the rapture or that we might be kicked out of the family. He emphasizes elsewhere that he knows he will be part of that. However, what he is afraid of here is missing out on the high calling or up-calling.

Those who are enemies of the cross of Christ are those who mind earthly things. They want to be seen of men as being successful or having authority in this life. The result will be that they will have their lives in the age to come destroyed because they will be found lacking at the Judgment Seat of Christ. The preaching of the cross is foolishness to them.[33]

The preaching of the cross is the power of God to us who are being saved! This has to do with the literal Millennial Kingdom of our Lord. This is one reason that many Bible teachers do not look at the underlying text. They have to abandon their preconceived ideas because they do not harmonize with what the text states. They do not want to believe in the accountability of the believer and they do not want to believe in a literal coming Kingdom where some will rule and reign and some will not.

What does this mean when it says, "to us who are being saved"? Acts 16:31 teaches that when we believe, we are in the family of God, and we will be there forever, and nothing can take us out of it. We will be in the family of God forever, just as Jesus will be in the family forever. But this passage is referring to those who are in the process of being saved. The process implies that we may not be in the sweet by and by unless we eventually get saved. If we are in the process, then we might not make it. This salvation is referring to rewards. Salvation has a past tense, a present tense, and a future tense. We have been saved, we are being saved, and we will be saved. What we can lose is not our born-from-above salvation, but we can lose rewards in the coming Kingdom. You may not be able to lose your common salvation, but you can lose your life in the coming age.[34]

---

[33] This is not to say that everyone who is successful or in authority in this life will miss out. You can be successful and still be faithful. The question is, where does your heart lie?

[34] See our book Warnings in Hebrews, Adoption, and Why We Are All Going to Hell which was mentioned earlier.

Perishing

[1 Corinthians 15:16-18: For if the dead are not raised, then Christ has not been raised. If Christ has not been raised, your faith is futile and you are still in your sins. Then those also who have died [fallen asleep] in Christ have perished.]

Have perished. They have lost their life, if Christ has not been raised from the dead. If Christ be not raised from the dead, we cannot know and experience the power of the resurrection. It takes the high priestly office of the Lord Jesus Christ for us to be overcomers. If Christ is not raised there is no resurrection and no overcoming, and our faith is in vain. It does not mean that we will be damned into the lake of fire prepared for the devil and his angels because he died that all men might be saved. But it means we will not rule and reign in the coming Kingdom with the Lord Jesus Christ.

Make no mistake: Believers can lose their life for the coming Kingdom. We cannot lose our place in the family; that is irrevocable. God does not want any to perish, but as we have seen, many *will* perish. We look forward to *the* promise, which has to do with life in the age to come. He wants us all to repent from dead works and sin. The wages of sin is death. The wages of sin in a believer's life will bring forth perishing. But he is long suffering. He is patient and he waits. He will put you in circumstances in life that make you think about him. He wants you to repent. He wants you to rule and reign in the coming age. You have to be faithful.

One thing we have been promised is that if we are faithful we are going to have trouble. We have also been warned that if we are not faithful, we are going to have trouble. You know you are going to have trouble. Prepare for trouble.

[1 Corinthians 9:24-27: Do you not know that in a race the runners all compete, but only one receives the prize? Run in such a way that you may win it. Athletes exercise self-control in all things; they do it to receive a perishable wreath, but we an imperishable one. So I do not run aimlessly, nor do I box as though beating the air; but I punish my body and enslave it [keep my body under subjection], so that after proclaiming to others I myself should not be disqualified.]

This is talking about a prize and we are warned we can become disqualified or disapproved. This brings us back to 1 Corinthians 10, which we touched on earlier.

[1 Corinthians 10a: I do not want you to be unaware, ~~brothers and sisters~~ brethren...]

Keep in mind to whom he is speaking. These who are being warned are in the family.

[1 Corinthians 10b-3: that our ancestors were all under the cloud, and all passed through the sea, and all were baptized into Moses in the cloud and in the sea, and all ate the same spiritual food...]

In verses 1-3, their ancestors all left Egypt, they were baptized in the sea and the cloud, and they ate of the same spiritual food. They were faithful and obedient. They were growing in grace and growing in the knowledge of the Lord. They were feeding upon God's Word.

[1 Corinthians 10:4: and all drank the same spiritual drink. For they drank from the spiritual rock that followed them, and the rock was Christ.]

They were partakers of the Holy Spirt. Water, in type, is representative of the Holy Spirit. They were made partakers of the Holy Spirit and this is a parallel to Hebrews 6.[35]

[1 Corinthians 10:5: Nevertheless, God was not pleased with most of them, and they were struck down in the wilderness.]

They were disapproved. That is Paul's fear.

[1 Corinthians 10:6: Now these things occurred as examples for us, so that we might not desire evil as they did.]

In chapter 9, Paul said, "but I punish my body and enslave it". The KJV says, "I keep my body under subjection. Bodily lusts were what caused the Children of Israel to complain and fail. We battle the world, the flesh, and the devil, and any one of those can cause us to perish. Let us not murmur against the Lord.

[1 Corinthians 10:7-9: Do not become idolaters as some of them did; as it is written, "The people sat down to eat and drink, and they rose up to play." We must not indulge in sexual immorality as some of them did, and twenty-three thousand fell in a single day. We must not put Christ to the test, as some of them did, and were destroyed [perished] by serpents.]

They were perished by serpents.

[1 Corinthians 10:10: And do not complain as some of them did, and were destroyed [perished] by the destroyer [exterminator; different word].]

---

[35] See Warnings in Hebrews, Adoption, and Why We Are All Going to Hell.

Serpents caused them to lose their lives. They did not get to enter into the land flowing with milk and honey, which is in type the Kingdom of the heavens. They were already in the land that was promised as an inheritance to Abraham, Isaac, and Jacob, based upon nothing but being in the family. But they would miss out on the better part of the inheritance, which is the land flowing with milk and honey that was promised based upon having a faithful walk.

We need to remember there are two Promised Lands: One based upon nothing but being in the family and the other based upon faithful service.

[Genesis 15:18: On that day the LORD made a covenant with Abram, saying, "To your descendants I give this land, from the river of Egypt [the Nile] to the great river, the river Euphrates.]

The Lord promised them the land from the Nile to the Euphrates, then follows it up with the land of ten tribes.[36] The number ten represents completeness and divine perfection. *All* the land from the Nile to the Euphrates was to be theirs, based upon simply being in the family.

Think about that for a moment. Before they even left Egypt, while they were still in the land of Goshen, which was to the east of the Nile, they were already in the land that was promised to Abraham, Isaac, and Jacob. They could have stayed in Egypt and perished and still had the inheritance that God had promised to Abraham, Isaac, and Jacob. Even though they were in their

---

[36] These ten tribes are also Nephilim tribes. They have populated the land in an attempt to thwart God's plans.

inheritance, they were not serving God, and that was the point. God wanted them to quit serving the world, the flesh, and the devil, and to come out into the desert to serve him. He wanted them to offer feasts unto him. And he wanted to try them and put them on probation to see if they would qualify to enter into a *better* inheritance, the Land Flowing with Milk and Honey.

We are not going to post all the passages about the Land Flowing with Milk and Honey, but you can begin in Exodus 3 and read about it. There are fourteen passages in the Torah that describes Israel as the Land Flowing with Milk and Honey. Fourteen is the number of deliverance or release.[37]

Just as Israel had two lands of inheritance, we have two inheritances offered to us. We can have a heavenly inheritance with heavenly blessings and positions of authority, or we can expect a worldly inheritance. Being denied an entrance into the Kingdom of the Heavens is what the worldly inheritance amounts to. It is the same choice the children of Israel had. They could inherit just like Dan, Reuben, and Gad, who stopped short of the best part and settled east of the Jordan River. Their inheritance was in the desert. Their inheritance was not in the Land Flowing with Milk and Honey. They were satisfied with second best. They were still in the Land of Promise, just not the better part.

[Genesis 22:17-18: I will indeed bless you, and I will make your offspring as numerous as the stars of heaven and as the sand that is on the seashore. And your offspring shall possess the gate of their enemies, and by your offspring shall all the nations of the

---

[37] The phrase "land flowing with milk and honey" appears fifteen times, but in Numbers 16:13, the rebels Dathan and Abiram use the phrase to describe Egypt.

87

earth gain blessing for themselves, because you have obeyed my voice."]

Abraham was promised an earthly seed (the sand of the seashore) and a heavenly seed (the stars of heaven). Two inheritances available.

It is just like Esau. Esau got a blessing. Esau got an inheritance. A lot of people think Esau did not get an inheritance at all. They think he lost everything. I have even heard that preached in the pulpit. But Isaac divided his goods into three portions and gave Jacob two of them, plus all the honor and responsibility that goes with the double portion and he gave the rest to Esau. Esau got an inheritance, but he forfeited the better inheritance.[38]

[Hebrews 11:20: By faith Isaac invoked blessings for the future on Jacob and Esau.]

They both received blessings, and those blessings concerned things to come, but Jacob esteemed the better inheritance. Although Jacob did not quite get his by faithfulness, he did repent and he eventually let God have control. We need to do that and have that experience with the Lord.

God's children perished in the wilderness and they did not enter into the better inheritance, which was in the Land Flowing with Milk and Honey.

[1 Corinthians 15:10: But by the grace of God I am what I am, and his grace toward me has not been in vain. On the contrary, I

---

[38] He was not too happy about the situation and he caused Jacob trouble for the rest of their lives.

worked harder than any of them—though it was not I, but the grace of God that is with me.]

Paul used the grace of God for profit. He put the grace of God into the things he did, in order that his works would be works of gold, silver, and precious stones. He wanted his service to be acceptable to God, and so God bestowed grace upon him, and it was not in vain. Why? "I worked harder than any of them." The KJV says, "But I labored more abundantly." The more grace that God gives, the more abundantly we can labor. We must have grace if we wish to serve God acceptably.

[Hebrews 12:28 KJV: Wherefore we receiving a kingdom which cannot be moved, let us have grace, whereby we may serve God acceptably with reverence and godly fear.]

[2 Corinthians 9:8 KJV: And God is able to make all grace abound toward you; that ye, always having all sufficiency in all things, may abound to every good work.]

[1 Corinthians 15:10b: Though it was not I, but the grace of God that is with me.]

The grace of God did the laboring. We have to do the work, but the grace of God is what makes it work.

[1 Corinthians 15:11-14: Whether then it was I or they, so we proclaim and so you have come to believe. Now if Christ is proclaimed [preached] as raised from the dead, how can some of you say there is no resurrection of the dead? If there is no resurrection of the dead, then Christ has not been raised; and if Christ has not been raised, then our proclamation [preaching] has been in vain [empty] and ~~your faith~~ *the* faith of you has been in vain [empty].]

Preaching has to do with labor. Faith is a lifestyle. The just shall live by faith. Those who will stand justified or righteous at the Judgment Seat of Christ and will have a full entrance into the coming Kingdom of the Heavens are those who live by faith. They are actively doing the will of the Father. They are living by *the* faith. There is the definite article with the word "faith": The faith of you is empty if there is no resurrection from among the dead.

[1 Corinthians 15:15-18: We are even found to be misrepresenting God, because we testified of God that he raised Christ—whom he did not raise if it is true that the dead are not raised. For if the dead are not raised, then Christ has not been raised. If Christ has not been raised, your faith is futile [fruitless; devoid of truth][39] and you are still in your sins. Then those also who have died [fallen asleep] in Christ have perished [*apollumi*].]

If Christ has not been raised. I want to remind you of what verses 1-4 says.

[1 Corinthians 15:1-4: Now I would remind you, brothers and sisters, of the good news that I proclaimed to you, which you in turn received, in which also you stand, through which also you are being saved, if you hold firmly to the message that I proclaimed to you—unless you have come to believe in vain [yet a different word; feignedly]. For I handed on to you as of first

---

[39] Some translations have the word "vain" here, but it is a different word than that found in verse 14 that is also translated as "vain". In verse 14, it is "empty"; in verse 17 it is "devoid of truth".

importance what I in turn had received: that Christ died for our sins in accordance with the scriptures, and that he was buried, and that he was raised on the third day in accordance with the scriptures...]

# What It Means To Lose The Life

# If We Hold Firmly to the Message

"If you hold firmly to the message…" If you retain or keep in memory the message he proclaimed…

This gospel message that Paul preached is conditional upon the fact that you have to keep it in memory. That does not mean to simply memorize it, but to put it into action.

[2 Peter 1:13: I think it right, as long as I am in this body, to refresh your memory [stir you up]…]

[2 Peter 3:1-2: This is now, beloved, the second letter I am writing to you; in them I am trying to arouse [stir up] your sincere intention [pure minds] by reminding you that you should remember the words spoken in the past by the holy prophets, and the commandment of the Lord and Savior spoken through your apostles.]

Peter talked about stirring up their minds to remembrance. We have to remember or hold firmly to the message.

[1 John 3:3: And all who have this hope in him purify themselves, just as he is pure.]

If we hold fast this message in our minds, then we will purify ourselves, even as he is pure, in order to prepare ourselves for an entrance into the coming Kingdom. That is our hope!

What message do we need to hold fast? "What I [Paul] preached to you, unless you have believed feignedly." What did he preach to them? He preached the gospel of the saving of the soul and an entrance into the Kingdom. "I gave you first that which I also received how Christ dies for our sins according to the Scriptures and he was buried, and he rose again the third day." Why did God raise him from among the dead? He was raised that our faith be not empty or wasted and of no value.

[1 Corinthians 15:17: If Christ has not been raised, your faith is futile and you are still in your sins.]

He is talking to those who have believed on the Lord Jesus Christ and that he died for the sins of the world. For us to be still in our sins means that we are yet under the subjection, servitude, and authority of sin in our life. Sin would be ruling in our lives if Jesus Christ had not been raised from the dead.

[Romans 6:11, 12, 14, 16: So you also must consider yourselves dead to sin and alive to God in Christ Jesus. Therefore, do not let sin exercise dominion in your mortal bodies, to make you obey their passions...For sin will have no dominion over you, since you are not under law but under grace...Do you not know that if you present yourselves to anyone as obedient slaves, you are slaves of the one whom you obey, either of sin, which leads to death, or of obedience, which leads to righteousness?]

This is what it means to still be in your sins. This is the righteousness of faith that Noah preached. If Christ is not raised from the dead, then sin still has dominion over us *because Jesus Christ is our high priest.* He is the one that ministers grace and power. It is his power, his might, his wisdom, his righteousness, his faith, and it is his grace. That is why the Lord Jesus Christ is at the right hand of God the father and that is the reason he is the high priest today, that we might have hope of entrance into the coming Kingdom. If he has not been raised, we have no power, no grace, and no hope!

[1 Corinthians 15:17: If Christ has not been raised, your faith is futile and you are still in your sins.]

***The faith***. It is not just "faith", it is a particular faith. There's the definite article before it. "The faith of you is futile and you are still in your sins."

[1 Corinthians 15:18: Then those also who have died [fallen asleep] in Christ have perished [*apollumi*].]

This is the good sense of having fallen asleep. This is the sleep that is passive. They are put to repose. This is the sleep that the Lord Jesus Christ puts his believers into when it is time to go home. When it is time to go home, as far as your life is concerned, it is a passive event. Jesus Christ is the one who puts his children to sleep. Even if we struggle, just as our babies did when they did not want to go to sleep and their eyes would roll up and they would fight it, we will be put into repose in Christ. We may struggle, but when it is time to go home, the Lord acts upon us actively and we are passive.

If Christ has not been raised, those believers who have already gone on have perished. They have lost their lives. They will not have entrance into the Kingdom of the Heavens. If Christ has not been raised, then they did not – they could not! – appropriate the high priestly office of the Lord Jesus Christ.

[1 Corinthians 15:19: If for this life only we have hoped in Christ, we are of all people most to be pitied.]

If he is not raised, we are of all people most to be pitied. We are of all men most miserable. Even though we have all this faithfulness, even though we are denying ourselves, even though we are taking up our cross, and even though we are doing the hard things, what a miserable life it would be if there was no hope of ruling and reigning with the Lord Jesus. It would be a waste! It would be a waste because there would be no grace involved, and if there were no grace involved, there would be no acceptable service. Jesus Christ was raised from among the dead and he is in the heavenlies in the tabernacle ministering for us. His blood is on the Mercy Seat for our deliverance and he is providing grace in order that our service may be acceptable.

In case you cannot stand the suspense, I will not leave you in a cliffhanger and I will give away the ending: Christ **_was_** raised from the dead. Never have any doubts. He is risen! Hallelujah!

[1 Corinthians 15:20: But in fact Christ has been raised from the dead, the first fruits of those who have died [fallen asleep].]

Here is the exhortation.

[1 Corinthians 15:34: Come to a sober and right mind [awake to righteousness], and sin no more; for some people have no knowledge of God. I say this to your shame.]

As Rotherham's states it, "Wake up to sobriety, in righteousness, and be not committing sin...

This word that is translated as "come to a sober and right mind" specifically means to awaken from a drunken stupor. It does not simply mean to get your mind right. It implies returning to righteousness. This righteousness is the righteousness which is by faith. This is the righteousness which Noah preached. This is the righteousness which is associate with the message Jesus gave his disciples.

[Matthew 5:20: For I tell you, unless your righteousness exceeds that of the scribes and Pharisees, you will never enter the kingdom of heaven.]

The scribes and Pharisees were righteous. They were the rabbis. The scribes were the small number of regular teachers and the Pharisees were... well, they were Pharisaical. But Jesus says unless your righteousness exceeds theirs you will not enter the Kingdom of the Heavens.

"Sober up to righteousness and quit sinning." This awaking to righteousness is associated with the knowledge (*epignOsis*; deeper knowledge) of God.

[Ephesians 5:13-14: but everything exposed by the light becomes visible, for everything that becomes visible is light. Therefore it says, "Sleeper, awake! Rise from the dead, and Christ will shine on you."]

Rise from among the dead ones! Arise! Wake up! Arise from among those Christians who have no entrance in ruling and reigning with the Lord Jesus Christ. They are perishing.

[1 Corinthians 1:18: For the message about the cross is foolishness to those who are perishing, but to us who are being saved it is the power of God.]

For those Christians who are perishing, the preaching of the cross to them is foolishness.

The word "perishing" is present and passive or middle voice and it is a present, participle. That means they are causing the action to happen to themselves, or the actions are happening to them and they are on the way to destruction. They are not helpless bystanders. God gives us these warnings and exhortations in order that we might realize the blessings God has for us. These are blessings God has prepared for those who love him, and those who love him keep his commandments. They are obedient. These exhortations are for those who will rule and reign in righteousness and shine as stars in the firmament of the heavens.

God is not willing that any of his children should lose their life for the coming age. His desire is that everyone might be saved and come to a knowledge of the truth and that knowledge pertains to his coming Kingdom and glory. Our preaching is not vain and our faith is not vain.

Faith is a lifestyle. The just shall live by faith. A life of faith is a life that will be found pleasing to the Lord.

[Hebrews 11:6: And without faith it is impossible to please God, for whoever would approach him must believe that he exists and that he rewards those who seek him.]

[Romans 5:2: through whom we have obtained access *by faith* to this grace in which we stand; and we let us boast in our *hope* of sharing the glory of God.]

Faith is necessary if we are to have the grace to serve him acceptably, and if we serve him acceptably, we can have the expectation of sharing in the glory of God.

# Perishing

If there is no resurrection our faith is futile and we are still dead in our sins. We preach the resurrection, and if the dead be not raised, we are false witnesses. In those days, a false witness was stoned to death. If there is no resurrection, we are still in our sins and we are perished.

[Romans 6:12: Therefore, do not let sin exercise dominion [reign] in your mortal bodies, to make you obey their passions.]

[Romans 6:4: Therefore have been buried with him by baptism into death, so that, just as Christ was raised from the dead by the glory of the Father, so we too might walk in newness of life.]

If we are to walk a clean life, we need the power of the resurrection! We need to be able to access the high priestly office of the Lord Jesus Christ. If Christ be not raised from among the dead, we do not have power over that sin, and we cannot be baptized and walk in newness of life.

But he has been raised!

[Philippians 3:8-9: More than that, I regard everything as loss because of the surpassing value of knowing Christ Jesus my Lord. For his sake I have suffered the loss of all things, and I regard them as rubbish, in order that I may gain Christ and be found in him, not having a righteousness of my own that comes from the law, but one that comes through faith in Christ, the righteousness from God based on faith.]

If Christ be not raised, the just do not live by faith. They **_cannot_** live by faith! This righteousness comes through faith in Christ and if Christ be not raised, our faith if in vain.

[Philippians 3:10a: I want to know Christ and the power of his resurrection...]

We need to have this faith for righteousness in order that we can have a personal relationship with him. This word "know" is not *epignOsis* [deeper knowledge], it is simply "know". It is personal acquaintance.

Why would Paul, who met the Lord Jesus face to face on the road to Damascus, then spent three years in the desert in Arabia being taught in a one-on-one basis say "I want to know Christ"? This is a personal servant of God who is more intimately acquainted with the Lord than almost anyone in history, hoping that he may know the Lord.

[Romans 10:17: So faith comes from what is heard, and what is heard comes through the word of Christ [or God].[40]]

The evidence of knowing the Lord is that we are spending time in fellowship with him by studying his word. Paul had the privilege of knowing him on a one-to-one personal basis and we can know him through the word as our faith is increased.

[Philippians 3:10-11: I want to know Christ and the power of his resurrection and the sharing of his sufferings by becoming like him in his death, if somehow I may attain the resurrection from the dead.]

---

[40] The difference between the "word of God" and the "word of Christ" is a very important distinction with deep theological implications. Some manuscripts have "God" and others have "Christ". We will not be going into that in this study, but will do so at a future date, Lord willing.

Perishing

"The power of his resurrection...." Paul knew the meaning and importance of the resurrection.

[Philippians 3:14: I press on toward the goal for the prize of the heavenly call of God in Christ Jesus.]

This out-resurrection has to do with the prize. A prize is something that is earned. This is the resurrection from among the dead ones. The dead ones are those whose lives have been perished because of unfaithfulness. This is the prize of the heavenly or upward calling.

In verse 10, "may attain" is subjunctive. There is no assurance he will reach the prize of which he is speaking.

[Philippians 3:12-13: Not that I have already obtained this or have already reached the goal; but I press on to make it my own, because Christ Jesus has made me his own. Beloved, I do not consider that I have made it my own; but this one thing I do: forgetting what lies behind and straining forward to what lies ahead.]

There is no assurance of the prize. We have assurance that we are in the family and that can never be taken away or even forfeited. We can, however, come up short of the prize. He "may attain". He has not already obtained this; he has not reached the goal. But he exhorts us to press on or strain forward.

[1 Peter 1:3: Blessed be the God and Father of our Lord Jesus Christ! By his great mercy he has given us a new birth [born again] into a living hope through the resurrection of Jesus Christ from the dead...]

We are born again into a ***living*** hope!

"Born again" is not the same as we find in John 3:3 in which we must be born from above in order to see the Kingdom. This is born again unto a ***living*** hope.[41]

A living hope is not dead. Peter uses this word quite a bit. The Pharisees held to the hope of the resurrection, but the resurrection of Jesus gave that hope permanence. It put meat on the bones of that hope, so to speak. It turned a dead hope into a living hope, just as we can turn a dead faith into a living faith. This living hope came by means of the resurrection.

[1 Peter 1:4-5: and into an inheritance that is imperishable, undefiled, and unfading, kept in heaven for you, who are being protected by the power of God through faith for a salvation ready to be revealed in the last time.]

The Lord Jesus Christ is at the right hand of God the Father that he might minister his blood to us for deliverance from the power of sin in our lives. Why? Because sin can reign in our lives and we need access to the blood. Sin can have control or dominion, and we need deliverance from that dominion.

There are those who falsely teach that sin cannot have dominion in the life of a believer.

[Romans 6:12: Therefore, do not let sin exercise dominion in your mortal bodies, to make you obey their passions.]

---

[41] See <u>Search the Scriptures</u> by the same author for a study on this subject.

If sin could not have dominion in the life of a believer, Paul would not warn believers about it. That would by contradictory and the Bible is not contradictory. Sin _can_ reign, therefore god made provision for us to have deliverance from anything that would bring us into captivity, whether it is the word, the flesh, or the devil. These things can enslave us and put us into bondage.

We must appropriate the power of the resurrection. We must walk in righteousness and sin not. We must practice right living and not let sin have dominion. We must appropriate our High Priest. If we do not, we will perish. If we do not approach the mercy seat, we will serve sin and we will serve the world. We will serve unto death. We will perish and lose our life in the age to come.

What It Means To Lose The Life

104

# The Mystery of Lawlessness

[2 Thessalonians 2:7: For the mystery of lawlessness is already at work, but only until the one who now restrains it is removed.]

The mystery of lawlessness.

This is a hard chapter. At least it is hard when you do not have all the answers. One day it will not be hard because the Lord will share it all with us.

This mystery of lawlessness is already at work when this was written. The KJV calls lawlessness "iniquity".[42] This mystery of lawlessness is not just in the world but is in the lives of believers.

[2 Thessalonians 2:3: Let no one deceive you in any way; for that day will not come unless the ~~rebellion~~ *the* apostasy [falling away] comes first and the lawless one [man of lawlessness] is revealed, ~~the one destined for destruction~~ the son of destruction.]

*The* man of *the* lawlessness, *the* son of *the* destruction.

There are definite articles with each word here. This is a man who is hidden and when the falling away comes, he will be revealed. This is not Satan but it is someone who is doing the work of Satan. When he is revealed, watch out!

---

[42] However, they did not translate it consistently, so sometimes they simply translate it as "sin".

105

These things will happen after *the* apostasy. This is not the world "falling away". You cannot fall away from somewhere you never were. This is referring to believers falling away from things they once held precious. This is the mystery of lawlessness.

Lawlessness has to do with having no respect for the law. It is doing what is right in one's own eyes. We are surrounded by lawlessness.[43] There is no respect for God's laws, even by those who are in the family. Believers, who should be setting the example, will fall away and become lawless! Many of them are lawless today.

[2 Thessalonians 2:7-8: For the mystery of lawlessness is already at work, but only until the one who now restrains it is removed. And then the lawless one will be revealed, whom the Lord Jesus will destroy [consume; not *apollumi*] with the breath of his mouth, annihilating him by the manifestation of his coming.]

This is the man of sin; the son of perdition. He will be destroyed and consumed. The devil will be thrown into the bottomless pit for a thousand years and the false prophet will be cast into the lake of fire.

[2 Thessalonians 2:9: The coming of the lawless one is apparent in the working of Satan, who uses all power, signs, lying wonders [false miracles]...]

---

[43] This would include the lawlessness of unjust laws. The world has turned the law on its head and calls good evil and evil good. There can be no crime without criminal intent, but there can be vice, which is sin but without the intent to invade the property or rights of another. To quote MLK (who misquoted Thomas Jefferson), "One has not only a legal but a moral responsibility to obey just laws. Conversely, one has a moral responsibility to disobey unjust laws."

Perishing

The lawless one will perform miracles. "Power, signs, and lying wonders..." through the power of Satan.

[2 Thessalonians 2:10: and every kind of wicked deception [seduction of unrighteousness] for those who are perishing [*apollumi*], because they refused to love *the* truth and so be saved.]

Those who are being perished. "Every kind of wicked deception..." Seduction of unrighteousness. Unrighteous is the negative of righteous or just. These are unjust. The just shall live by faith. The unjust (believers) will have no inheritance in the coming Kingdom.[44]

These who are perishing are those who refused to love *the* truth. This is beyond simply being born from above. This salvation has to do with life in the age to come.[45]

[2 Thessalonians 2:14: For this purpose he called you through our proclamation of the good news, so that you may obtain the glory of our Lord Jesus Christ.]

---

[44] The just are like Elizabeth and Zechariah in Luke 1. They were blameless as far as the covenants and the ordinances of the Lord; they were obedient unto the Lord.
[45] There are many who teach that these people who refused to love the truth and be saved are tribulation saints. They teach that those who hear the gospel today and reject it will not have a chance to be saved. That is incorrect. The only sin that will not be forgiven is blasphemy of the Holy Spirit. Anything done or said against the Lord Jesus Christ will be forgiven because that is the nature of his work. People will be able to be saved during the tribulation period.

The obtaining of the glory of our Lord Jesus Christ is the salvation referred to in verse 10.

[2 Thessalonians 2:16: Now may our Lord Jesus Christ himself and God our Father, who loved us and through grace gave us eternal [*aionian*] comfort and good hope through grace…]

This word "comfort" is the Greek word for "calling" with the prefix "*para*" attached to it [*paraklEsis*]. When you attach a preposition to a verb it intensifies the verb. This is an extreme or earnest calling and good hope through grace.

This earnest calling is to the obtaining of the glory. The hope is Christ in you, the hope of glory. The obtaining of the glory will only be realized through God's grace. If you do not have grace in your life when you are serving the Lord, your works will not be acceptable when you stand at the Judgment Seat of Christ.

These people who can be deceived by power, signs, and false miracles are those who reject Kingdom truths and doctrines. They are believers, but they will perish and will not have what they expect in the coming Kingdom.

[Matthew 24:24: For false messiahs and false prophets will appear and produce great signs and omens, to lead astray, if possible, even the elect.]

These false prophets and messiahs will be performing miracles that will be amazing! But let us not forget, signs and wonders do not, by themselves prove holiness. They will deceive many. The implication here is that it is impossible to deceive the elect, or the called out ones, but many will be deceived, even believers.

# Perishing

[Matthew 7:21a: "Not everyone who says to me, 'Lord, Lord,' will enter the kingdom of heaven, but only the one who does the will of my Father in heaven.]

This has to do with an entrance into the Kingdom, not just seeing. To be born from above, all you do is believe and you will see the Kingdom. But an entrance is based upon doing the will of the Father.

What things are not the will of the father?

[Matthew 7:22: On that day many will say to me, 'Lord, Lord, did we not prophesy in your name, and cast out demons in your name, and do many deeds of power in your name?']

These people prophesied in his name. When they said, "Did we not do these things in your name?" he had the opportunity to say, "No, you did not!" They were foretelling the future and giving extra revelations from God. Do you see people doing that today? They were casting out demon and they were working miracles.

[Matthew 7:23: Then I will declare to them, 'I never knew you; go away from me, you evildoers.']⁴⁶

---

[46] "I thought he knew everything! This is a contradiction!" He does know everything. However, this word is used as a means of declaring intimacy, not simply a basic knowledge. They were declaring an intimacy with him and he said, "Not true!"

As an example of the usage of the word "know" in this way, refer to 1 Kings 1:1-4 in which King David was old and could not get warm so they sent for a young damsel to keep him warm. They knew everything about her, yet verse 4 says, "He knew her not". Some translations interpret the meaning in that

Notice, he did not say, "You were not doing those things in my name!"

They are evildoers. The KJV says, "Depart from me, ye that work iniquity". They were practicing lawlessness. They are workers of lawlessness. They do not know the Word of God or the will of God. They are interested in sensual and external signs, wonders, and miracles. They wanted excitement, so they created it!

"To lead astray, if possible, even the elect."

The elect are those who will rule and reign with the Lord Jesus in the coming Kingdom. They are the ones who are called out from among the called. The elect will not be deceived by things. These are things of Satan.

Remember, Satan is an angel of light. He is trying to deceive believers to get them to do things that are not the will of God. He does not need to deceive non-believers. He would try to deceive us into seeking after things that are not the will of God. He does not want atheists, he wants religious people who can be deceived. He wants you to seek after signs, wonders, and miracles. He wants you to seek after the sign-gifts such as speaking in tongues, visions, healing, raising the dead, etc. These things are not for today, but they are exciting and they tug on a believer's heart when they see these things. Why? Because he knows that if we seek after these things we will be disqualified from entering. Satan's ambition and desire is to defeat us in our Christian life. A wicked and adulterous generation seeks after signs.

---

verse, whereas they simply translate in Matthew 7:23. (And I, for one, would like to see the job application for keeping the king warm.)

Perishing

Believers who know Kingdom truths will get involved in these things and then they lose interest in things pertaining to the Kingdom. They are more interested in things that are soulish and exciting. There are people who speak in tongues and claim to be translated to different places just as Peter was and preaching and being translated back. These things are exciting and they stir up curiosity. Or it makes the hair stand up on the back of your head. Those who seek to do these things will not have an entrance, and having an entrance is what we need to be interested in. Do not be deceived by soulish things.

Satan is deceiving believers today. These people are not casting out demons by the power of Satan. Jesus stated that Satan cannot cast out himself. The Kingdom that casts itself out is divided and that kingdom will not stand. The way these gifts are operating today is the story of quail and kings.

These miracles and signs that these people are doing are similar to the quail in the Bible, in type. God wanted them to eat manna, but they wanted meat! The children of Israel wanted quail so much they pestered God until he gave it to them. God gave them something he did not want them to have and it made them sick. Numbers 11:20 tells us that it ran out their noses.

That is what is going on with tongues today. Many people are seeking after something that is not part of God's perfect plan, and he gives it to them and it makes them sick! Just like in the Desert, God wanted the people to eat manna and the people wanted something else.

Do not, however, make the mistake of assuming that just because it is not part of God's plan, it is demonic. If someone is "speaking

111

in tongues", are they using it the way God intended?[47] I have witnessed examples that **were** demonic. One person was speaking in tongues, another was "interpreting", and an out-of-country guest said, "They are speaking my language and that is not what they are saying; they are cursing God."[48] Sometimes they are simply spouting gibberish. But sometimes they may be doing it in the name of Lord, but under their own power, and it is lawlessness.

Miracles do happen today. However, a miracle by the direct hand of God is not the same thing that is being warned against. I know three people who were healed from cancer miraculously. I myself was the recipient of a miraculous event that defies any natural explanation. But these events were directly from God, not from the gifts of laying on of hands or signs that were being sought after.

At the Judgment Seat of Christ, signs, wonders, and miracles are going to come out of the noses of believers who stand there and see their life that they could have had in the coming Kingdom being taken from them. I guarantee you that they will be sick.

The anguish, tears, and disappointment that the children of Israel had when they got a king like Saul was a bitter experience. The Lord wanted to reign over them, but they wanted a king like the nations around them. God told Samuel, "Give them what they ask for". They picked a king based upon his good looks, not the

---

[47] Speaking In Tongues: Seven Crucial Questions by Joseph Dillow covers the biblical use of tongues very well.

[48] Sadly, those in attendance were so into the soulishness of events that they simply dismissed that as an aberration or a mistake, and continued carrying on.

content of his character. They got the king they wanted instead of living by God's will.

Be careful what you ask for because you just might get it!

[2 Thessalonians 2:9-10: The coming of the lawless one is apparent in the working of Satan, who uses all power, signs, lying wonders, and every kind of wicked deception for those who are perishing, because they refused to love the truth and so be saved.]

Those who are perishing refused to love the truth. God will let them go on and be deceived and in the end they will not rule and reign. He lets them go on and turns them over into captivity to the world, the flesh, and the devil.

Brethren, love the truth! Do not be deceived. Do not give up your life in the age to come for a little immediate gratification in this life. This is God's admonition to us.

Those of us who disqualify ourselves because of unfaithfulness will have a lot of weeping and gnashing of teeth, because of the disappointment of missing out on ruling and reigning with the Lord.

Perishing is to lose one's life. *Apollumi*. It is failing to obtain what you expect. It is a destruction from the presence of the Lord and the glory of his power in the age to come. *Aionios*. It does not mean total annihilation.

[2 Peter 3:6: through which the world of that time was deluged with water and perished [*apollumi*].]

The world did not become extinct. In fact, it was renewed.

[Hebrews 1:11-12: (the heavens; referring back to verse 10) they will perish [*apollumi*], but you remain; they will all wear out like clothing; like a cloak you will roll them up and like clothing they will be changed. But you are the same, and your years will never end.]

This passage is quoted from Psalm 102:25-27, and the heavens and the earth are compared with the eternity of God. "They shall perish". *Apollumi*. Notice the perishing is only preparatory to change and renewal. "They shall be changed."

Love the truth, love the Lord, and be faithful, and you will not perish.

# John 3:16 Revisited

Since we started with the most famous – and one of the most misused – verse in the Bible, John 3:16, we are going to conclude with a study of this verse.

[John 3:16: For God so loved the world, that he gave his only begotten Son, that whosoever believeth in him should not perish, but have everlasting [*aionian*] life.]

The first half of this verse is fairly simple and straightforward. It tells us what God had done for mankind. The second half is not so simple and this has misused and abused by many well-intentioned people over the years. In order to understand the second part of the verse, we need to take a look at the first part.

God. Who is the God who so love the world?

[Genesis 1:1: In the beginning when God created the heavens and the earth.]

[1 Peter 1:21: Through him you have come to trust in God, who raised him from the dead and gave him glory, so that your faith and hope are set on God.]

[Romans 3:29-30: Or is God the God of Jews only? Is he not the God of Gentiles also? Yes, of Gentiles also, since God is one; and he will justify the circumcised on the ground of faith and the uncircumcised through that same faith.]

God is in the beginning, he raised Jesus from the dead that your faith and hope might be in God, and he is the God of both the Jews and the Gentiles.

He so loved the world. The adverb "so" means "in this way". "For in this way, God loved the world."

[Ephesians 2:4: But God, who is rich in mercy, out of the **great love with which he loved us**...]

The verb "loved" is aorist, active, indicative in both John 3:16 and Ephesians 2:4. It is punctiliar action. It is an event. It is usually translated in the past tense, but the aorist simply indicates it is an event at a point in time. "God loved." He did this on purpose. He did not simply love with words, he put it into action: He gave his son.

"God Gave." God gave Jesus Christ to die for the sins of the world. "gave" is also aorist, active, indicative. It is punctiliar action. If you were to graph the aorist, you would use a dot on a timeline.

[Hebrews 9:26: for then he would have had to suffer again and again since the foundation of the world. But as it is, he has appeared once for all **at the end of the age** [aion] to remove sin by the sacrifice of himself.]

[Romans 5:8: But God proves his love for us in that while we still were sinners Christ died for us.]

[John 1:29: The next day he saw Jesus coming toward him and declared, "Here is the Lamb of God who takes away the sin of the world!]

Perishing

Jesus Christ saves those who believe on him as their personal savior, just as Nicodemus did in John 3:3.

[John 3:3: Jesus answered him, "Very truly, I tell you, no one can see the kingdom of God without being *born from above*."]

The verb "born" is aorist, passive, subjunctive. To be born into the world is an event that can only happen once. To born from above into the family of God is an event that can only happen once.[49]

[Acts 16:31: They answered, "Believe on the Lord Jesus, and you will be saved, you and your household."]

"Believe" is an aorist verb. This is an event. If one could forfeit salvation, the present tense would be used. In other words, if you believe as an event, this *will* happen. If the present tense had been used, it would say, "as long as you continue believing, this will happen".

"Believe" in Acts 16:31 and "born" in John 3:3 are both events.

"God gave." God also gave his son to be our High Priest.

[Hebrews 5:5-6: So also Christ did not glorify himself in becoming a *high priest*, but was appointed by the one who said to him, "You are my Son, *today I have begotten you*"; as he says

---

[49] Hence, the importance of being "born again" that is illustrated in 1 Peter and John 3:5. See our book Search the Scriptures for a more detailed study on this subject.

117

also in another place, "You are a ***priest*** forever [*aion*; age], according to the order of Melchizedek."]

[Hebrews 9:11: But when Christ came as a ***high priest*** of the ~~good things that have come~~ ***good things to come***, then through the greater and perfect tent (not made with hands, that is, not of this creation).]

[Romans 8:34: Who is to condemn? It is Christ Jesus, who ***died***, yes, who was ***raised***, who is ***at the right hand of God***, who indeed ***intercedes for us***.]

"For God so loved the world, that he gave his only begotten Son, **that**..."

The word "that" is translated from the word *ina* that could also be translated as "in order that".
In order that those who have been born from above and are being faithful to the Lord might hold fast to their profession.

[Hebrews 4:14: Since, then, we have a great high priest who has passed through the heavens, Jesus, the Son of God, let us ***hold fast*** to our confession.]

[Hebrews 10:23: Let us ***hold fast*** to the confession of our hope without wavering, for he who has promised is faithful.]

"...that whosoever believeth in him..."

The word "believeth" is a present, active, participle.[50] It is in the nominative case and has the definite article, so it is treated as a noun. The present tense of the verb "believe" is synonymous with the noun "faith", which is a lifestyle, not an action. These are the ones who are living by faith and are being faithful to the Lord.

[Acts 13:39: by this Jesus everyone who believes [present, active, participle] is ~~set free~~ justified [present, passive, indicative] from all those sins from which you could not be ~~freed~~ justified by the law of Moses.]

This verse is a typical Greek sentence which has its main clause at the end of the verse, which sounds odd to English ears, so the translators of the NRSV and KJV switched it around. The CLV has it as it is in the underlying text.

[Acts 13:39 CLV: and from all from which you could not be justified [aorist; an event] in the law of Moses, in this One [Jesus] everyone who is believing is being justified.]

[Romans 3:28: For we hold that a person is justified by faith apart from works prescribed by the law.]

To live by faith is to be believing in the present tense (actively) and that action can be stopped at any time. The action of the aorist tense of the verb "believe", as used in Acts 16:31 cannot be stopped or reversed because it is an event.

---

[50] The KJV translators used the –eth suffix to denote a present, active, participle, but they did not do it consistently. In modern English we would call this a gerund and it usually has the suffix –ing. In this case, it is "the one who is believing" in the present tense.

[Luke 8:13: The ones on the rock are those who, when they hear the word, receive [present, middle] it with joy. But these have [present, active] no root; they believe [present, active] only for a while and in a time of testing fall away [present, active].]

Remember, the middle voice means that it is something one causes to happen to oneself. They voluntarily receive.

The ones who are believing are the ones who continue to hear and they become rooted and grounded in the Word of God. Because they are grounded, they can remain faithful and they do not fall away when they are tested. They are able to endure. When a child of God stops believing, then he starts falling away and the process of justification also stops.[51] If you fall away, you become chargeable before God.

"…should not perish…"

In this verse, the word for "not" is μη. In the Greek, there are two words for not, ου and μη. The word μη is the milder negative. It is the word you would use when you do not want to be too positive about being negative. It is a hesitant negative. "I probably won't buy any more books." It leaves the door open. ου slams the door closed. (When you see them together, ου μη, it slams the door closed and nails it shut.) ου is objective and emphatic, dealing with fact, and μη is subjective and indefinite, dealing with thought.

---

[51] Justification, like salvation, is both an event and a process. We are justified when we are born from above into the family of God for our common salvation, but we have to continuously cause ourselves to be justified through our behavior for rewards.

# Perishing

Not perishing is dependent upon the faithfulness of the one who is believing. If you are believing (faithful), you should not perish. If you stop believing you may perish.

"Should perish" is from the word *apollumi*, and it is aorist, active, subjunctive. You cannot lose a life if you do not have a life to lose. Only those who are whole can be marred. Those who are already dead in their trespasses and sins cannot perish.

[John 3:14-15: And just as Moses lifted up the serpent in the wilderness, so must the Son of Man be lifted up, that whoever believes [present, active, participle] in him may have [present, active, subjunctive] eternal life.]

John 3:14-15 is the context of John 3:16.

This is referring to the events that happened in Numbers 21 which we looked at earlier. 1 Corinthians 10:11 tells us these events were given as types or examples.

[Numbers 34:2: Command the Israelites, and say to them: When you enter the land of Canaan (this is the land that shall fall to you for an inheritance, the land of Canaan, defined by its boundaries)]

They were made this promise based upon their faithfulness. All who perished in the wilderness lost their inheritance in the land flowing with milk and honey, which is the better inheritance.

All this happened to them and it is given to us to teach us that we can lose our reward (the better inheritance) because of the way we live. We will still have our fire insurance, but we will not have our full allotment!

[Colossians 3:24: since you know that from the Lord you will receive [get back] the inheritance as your reward [compensation or return]; you serve the Lord Christ.]

[2 John 1:8: Be on your guard, so that you do not lose [apollumi] what we [or you] have worked for [this is works!], but may receive a full reward [wages].]

This is talking about receiving wages based upon the works you have done. You cannot lose your common born-from-above salvation, but you *can* lose out on your inheritance. If you perish in this age, you can enjoy your wages or your inheritance in the coming age.

[Matthew 16:24-27: Then Jesus told his disciples [not unsaved people], "If any want to become my followers, let them **_deny themselves_** and take up their cross and follow me. For those who want to save their life [soul] will lose [apollumi] it, and those who lose [apollumi] their life [soul] for my sake will find it. For what will it profit them if they gain the whole world but forfeit [apollumi] their life [soul]? Or what will they give in return for their life [soul]? "For the Son of Man is to come with his angels in the glory of his Father, and then he will **_repay everyone for what has been done._**]

This is works. This is what we have earned. The wages of sin is death. The wages of faithful living is life in the age to come. We will receive the reward of our inheritance when Jesus comes in the glory of the Father with his angels. We can perish now and have rewards then or we can choose to not perish now and lose our rewards then. We can miss out on our potential life in the age to come because it will perish.

"...but may have..."

The verb "have" is present, active, subjunctive. The one who is believing on him may have *aionian* life. The one who is believing may stop believing. If we continue believing, we will have *aionian* life. But if we are believing for a while (faithful) and then stop, we will start losing our inheritance in the coming age. We will begin perishing.[52]

"...eternal life..."

We looked at what this word "everlasting" or "eternal" means earlier. It is *aionian* life. Life in the age to come. ***Having*** *aionian* life is the opposite of perishing. It is having a full allotment in the age to come. It is an adjective, which describes a person, place, or thing.[53]

[Mark 10:29-30: Jesus said, "Truly I tell you, there is no one who has left house or brothers or sisters or mother or father or children or fields, for my sake and for the sake of the good news [works], who will not receive a hundredfold now in this age—houses, brothers and sisters, mothers and children, and fields, with persecutions—and in the age [*aiOn*] to come eternal [*aionian*] life.]

[Matthew 19:28-29: Jesus said to them, "Truly I tell you, at the renewal of all things, when the Son of Man is seated on the throne of his glory, you who have followed me [works] will also sit on twelve thrones, judging the twelve tribes of Israel. And everyone

---

[52]The loss of reward does not happen suddenly, it is gradual.
[53] See Appendix 1.

who has left houses or brothers or sisters or father or mother or children or fields, for my name's sake, will receive a hundredfold, and will inherit eternal [*aionian*] life.]

When they inherit *aionian* life is when they will be ruling over the twelve tribes of Israel. It is the time when Christ will be sitting upon the throne of his glory. It is the thousand year reign of Christ. It is the millennial age.

Our inheritance is dependent upon what we do in this age. It is based upon works. We can perish in this age and live in the age to come or we can live in this age and perish in the Millennium.

[Romans 2:6-8: For he will repay ***according to each one's deeds***: to those who by patiently ***doing good*** seek for glory and honor and immortality, he will give eternal [*aionian*] life; while for those who are self-seeking and who obey not the truth but wickedness, there will be wrath and fury.]

It is through doing good that we are rewarded *aionian* life. Those who are wicked will be rewarded with wrath and fury.

[Galatians 6:7-9: Do not be deceived; God is not mocked, for ***you reap whatever you sow***. If you ***sow to your own flesh***, you ***will reap corruption*** from the flesh; but if you ***sow to the Spirit***, you ***will reap eternal [aionian] life*** from the Spirit. So let us not grow weary in doing what is right, for we ***will reap at harvest time, if we do not give up***.]

The idea is not giving up, but the words are, "If we faint not". If we faint, we will perish, but if we continue in faithfulness, we will reap *aionian* life.

# Perishing

[2 Timothy 2:12-13: if we _**endure**_ [present, active], we will also reign with him; if we deny him, he will also deny us; if we are _**faithless**_ [disbelieving; present tense], he remains faithful—for he cannot deny himself.]

We will reign if we remain faithful. It we are faithless, we will perish. Still in the family, but missing out on all that we could have.

Perishing is not having what one expects. It does not mean ultimate annihilation of being kicked out of the family, but it does mean missing out on all God wants you to have. If you perish, there will be great sorrow and weeping.

I want each of us to one day hear "well done", and just as Paul prayed, "_I pray God_ your whole spirit and soul and body be preserved blameless unto the coming of our Lord Jesus Christ."

# What It Means To Lose The Life

# Appendix 1

## Eternal Life

When studying, it is important to remember that there are many English words that have changed meaning over the years since the KJV was translated, and often, modern translations will keep the same word even if it has changed meaning. Also, some English words have a different meaning in Great Britain than in the United States. Some examples of words to keep in mind are adoption, conversation, and perhaps most importantly, eternal, everlasting, and similar words such as forever.

The English word "eternal" comes from the French *eterne*, which in turn comes from Latin *aeternalis*, which literally means "of great age". *Aionios* means "age-lasting" or can refer to the quality of something; but in no sense can it mean "forever and ever" the way we use it today. (By the same token, "forever" comes from the Old English through proto-German for "for an age".)

The word itself, "*aionios*", is an adjective that is formed from the noun "*aion*" which means "age". The meaning of an adjective cannot exceed the meaning of the noun from which it is formed. Hence, *aionios* is of limited duration.

New Testament eternity (in the modern meaning) is expressed in the phrase εις τους αιωνας των αιωνων, which is found in Galatians 1:5, and not in a single Greek word. Translated "unto to the ages of/from the ages." Some other examples are found in Philippians 4:20, 1 Timothy 1:17, 2 Timothy, 4:18 Hebrews 13:21, and 1 Peter 4:11.

A portion of all proceeds goes to help ministries around the world.